**Some typical hard disk sizes and their characteristics.**

| Disk size | Heads | Cylinders | Sectors/track | Disk size | Heads | Cylinders | Sectors/track |
|---|---|---|---|---|---|---|---|
| 10Mb | 4 | 306 | 17 | 71Mb | 10 | 823 | 17 |
| 21Mb | 3 | 820 | 17 | 71Mb | 8 | 1024 | 17 |
| 21Mb | 4 | 612 | 17 | 72Mb | 9 | 925 | 17 |
| 21Mb | 4 | 615 | 17 | 72Mb | 11 | 754 | 17 |
| 21Mb | 4 | 615 | 17 | 72Mb | 10 | 830 | 17 |
| 21Mb | 8 | 306 | 17 | 80Mb | 9 | 1024 | 17 |
| 25Mb | 3 | 987 | 17 | 85Mb | 5 | 969 | 36 |
| 31Mb | 5 | 733 | 17 | 88Mb | 4 | 1245 | 36 |
| 31Mb | 5 | 733 | 17 | 88Mb | 4 | 1249 | 36 |
| 31Mb | 5 | 733 | 17 | 98Mb | 11 | 1024 | 17 |
| 31Mb | 6 | 615 | 17 | 115Mb | 15 | 900 | 17 |
| 31Mb | 8 | 462 | 17 | 115Mb | 15 | 917 | 17 |
| 36Mb | 5 | 855 | 17 | 128Mb | 8 | 966 | 34 |
| 40Mb | 6 | 809 | 17 | 133Mb | 15 | 1024 | 17 |
| 42Mb | 5 | 977 | 17 | 137Mb | 10 | 823 | 34 |
| 42Mb | 5 | 977 | 17 | 144Mb | 8 | 1024 | 36 |
| 42Mb | 5 | 981 | 17 | 144Mb | 9 | 966 | 34 |
| 42Mb | 6 | 820 | 17 | 151Mb | 7 | 1225 | 36 |
| 42Mb | 7 | 699 | 17 | 151Mb | 7 | 1224 | 36 |
| 42Mb | 7 | 733 | 17 | 153Mb | 7 | 1245 | 36 |
| 42Mb | 8 | 615 | 17 | 153Mb | 9 | 969 | 36 |
| 44Mb | 5 | 1024 | 17 | 154Mb | 7 | 1249 | 36 |
| 44Mb | 7 | 733 | 17 | 159Mb | 15 | 1224 | 17 |
| 46Mb | 7 | 754 | 17 | 161Mb | 8 | 1147 | 36 |
| 48Mb | 6 | 940 | 17 | 166Mb | 8 | 1216 | 35 |
| 50Mb | 7 | 830 | 17 | 223Mb | 9 | 1412 | 36 |
| 51Mb | 5 | 989 | 17 | 249Mb | 12 | 1216 | 35 |
| 51Mb | 7 | 855 | 17 | 321Mb | 15 | 1218 | 36 |
| 55Mb | 7 | 918 | 17 | 323Mb | 15 | 1224 | 36 |
| 56Mb | 7 | 925 | 17 | 323Mb | 15 | 1225 | 36 |
| 58Mb | 7 | 977 | 17 | 372Mb | 15 | 1412 | 36 |
| 60Mb | 7 | 1024 | 17 | | | | |
| 61Mb | 7 | 1024 | 17 | | | | |
| 64Mb | 8 | 940 | 17 | | | | |

# Easy PC Maintenance and Repair

To my father Phillip Laplante

# Easy PC Maintenance and Repair

**Phil Laplante**

Windcrest®/McGraw-Hill

## Notices

| | |
|---|---|
| **HELPME**™ | California Software Products |
| **MS-DOS®, Windows**™ | Microsoft Corporation |
| **Norton Utilities®, Norton Backup**™ | Peter Norton Computing |
| **IBM Scan**™<br>**PC**™, **XT**™, **AT**™<br>**PC-DOS**™ | International Business Machines, Inc. |
| **PC Tools Deluxe**™ | Central Point Software |
| **Pro-Scan**™, **ViruScan**™ | McAfee Associates |
| **SpinRite**™ | Gibson Research |
| **UNIX®** | AT&T |
| **VirexPC**™ | MicroCom |

FIRST EDITION
FIFTH PRINTING



**Library of Congress Cataloging-in-Publication Data**

Laplante, Phil.
Easy PC maintenance and repair / by Phil Laplante.
p. cm.
ISBN 0-8306-3952-7 ISBN 0-8306-3953-5 (pbk.)
1. Microcomputers—Maintenance and repair. I. Title.
TK7887.L36 1992
621.39′16—dc20 91-35945
CIP

Acquisitions Editor: Roland S. Phelps
Managing Editor: Sandra L. Johnson
Book Editor: Susan J. Bonthron
Director of Production: Katherine G. Brown
Book Design: Jaclyn J. Boone
Paperbound Cover: Sandra Blair Design and
Brent Blair Photography, Harrisburg, Pa. EL1

# Contents

Acknowledgments

I would like to take this opportunity to thank the following friends and colleagues for revising the manuscript at various draft stages for technical accuracy and clarity:

Gary Birkmaier
Mike Crumrine
Dan Kopp
Armand Matejunas
Purnendu Sinha
Hiren Vakharia

Special thanks to Rob Martin who contributed significantly to the material. Also special thanks to Ken Snyder for his photographs. Any errors remaining in the text are, of course, mine.

# Introduction

If you own an IBM PC, XT, AT, or clone, you will want to maintain your investment, upgrade its capabilities, or repair it if it's broken. Commercial computer service centers are expensive and intimidating. Yet the average PC user can provide ongoing maintenance, upgrade, and even fix a difficult problem at home with basic tools. This book is designed to demystify the inner workings of the PC and to provide simple strategies for maintenance, repair, and upgrade that everyone can use. It also supplements the sometimes confusing installation manual that comes with your computers.

I wrote this book for owners of personal computers who wish to maintain, upgrade, or repair their computers themselves. I assume that you have run programs on PCs and are familiar with the DOS operating system, but I do not assume that you are knowledgeable about electronics or software technology.

You will particularly benefit from this text if any of the following apply to you:

- You have a personal computer at home.
- You are responsible for the upkeep of computer equipment at the office.
- You are a student or teacher in high school or college using the IBM PC, XT, AT, or clones in your class.
- You are a student or teacher in an adult education training program centered on PCs.

- You want to learn the basics of computer hardware and software technology.
- You are interested in advanced computer troubleshooting. (This book is a good starting point.)
- You want to learn how the IBM PC family of computers functions.

Although several books on the repair and maintenance of the PC are on the market, this book differs from them in a number of ways. It does not require any previous knowledge of electronics or software design. Nor is any special mathematical background needed. It assumes the reader has access only to basic tools such as screwdrivers and pliers. The book provides simple, step-by-step instructions for the troubleshooting, maintenance, and repair of the IBM PC, XT, AT, and their clones, and is not cluttered with unnecessary pricing or other information often used as filler. Specific instructions for a particular brand of computer are not given—the directions are as generic as possible so that owners of all PC computers can benefit. The text is enhanced by extensive tables, lists, photographs, and figures for clarity.

In addition, the book provides other benefits to the reader. It serves as an excellent introduction to the terminology associated with the PC and the basic concepts of computer architecture, and can serve as an introduction to the more advanced books on computer repair. It provides descriptions of selected commercial software products used in the troubleshooting and maintenance of PCs, and includes a discussion of computer viruses and their prevention. The book's material is ordered by increasing level of difficulty so that experienced readers can skip early sections. The book is self-contained—other than the documentation that came with your computer or computer parts, you won't need any other books. A comprehensive glossary of terms is included to assist in your understanding.

## How to use this book

This book is a supplement to your PC's hardware manual or the documentation accompanying any new computer parts you have purchased.

Before doing any modifications to the computer, you should fully read the appropriate section of this book, and your computer's installation guide. Better still, read both books first. In case of a conflict in advice, follow your computer's documentation. After you have had some time to think things over, you are ready to begin working on your computer. Be careful and patient, and you can surely succeed in prolonging the effective life of your computer while saving hundreds of dollars.

## About the author

Phil Laplante has been involved in computing for the last ten years as a programmer, consultant, and educator. He has extensive experience developing software in the UNIX, DOS, and other environments on various microcomputers. In addition, Dr. Laplante has been a consultant to many corporate clients in New Jersey on the repair and maintenance of microcomputers.

He holds a Ph.D. in electrical engineering and computer science from The Stevens Institute of Technology and is currently an Assistant Professor of Computer Science at Fairleigh Dickinson University. He has authored or coauthored over a dozen publications in magazines and technical journals. He is a licensed professional engineer in the state of New Jersey and a member of several professional and scientific organizations.

## Disclaimer

The author and publisher cannot be responsible for any damage or loss of computer data or time due to information contained in this book. Nor are the author and publisher responsible for the performance of any of the products mentioned in this book. The book is not intended for use as a factory repair manual for any specific machine.

## Conventions used in this book

For clarity of presentation, several conventions are used throughout the book.

- DOS commands are in an `alternate font`.
- Screen output from the computer is in an `alternate font`.
- All DOS commands, unless otherwise noted, end by pressing the Enter key.
- New terminology appears in italic type.
- Throughout the text, DOS is used as shorthand notation for *disk operating system*.
- Items of interest to advanced users are usually classified as a **NOTE**.
- Information that is critical to the safety of the user, computer, or data is indicated as a **WARNING!**.
- In the troubleshooting sections, the strategies are listed in the order in which you should try them.

Every attempt has been made to define terms before they are used. An extensive glossary has also been provided for your reference.

# Chapter 1

# Parts of the PC

This chapter conducts a brief tour of the basic components of the generic IBM PC as shown in Fig. 1-1. I examine each of these components in detail later when I discuss their replacement and repair. Note that Fig. 1-1 shows the computer with its cover removed.

## Removing the cover

Typically cover removal involves the following steps:

1. Unplug the computer. Move the computer to a clean, well-lighted, and safe work area. Place the monitor to the side of the system unit.
2. Loosen and remove the screws securing the cover to the computer chassis (e.g., on IBM PCs there are four screws, two on each side).
3. Slide the cover away from the chassis. In many cases the cover is held tightly in place, and may require a slight tug to free it. Be sure all necessary screws have been removed before attempting to force the cover off.
4. Put the screws aside in a safe place.
5. With a dust cloth, wipe away any dust that may have collected on the inside of the cover. Then put the cover out of your way.
6. To replace the cover, reverse steps three and two.

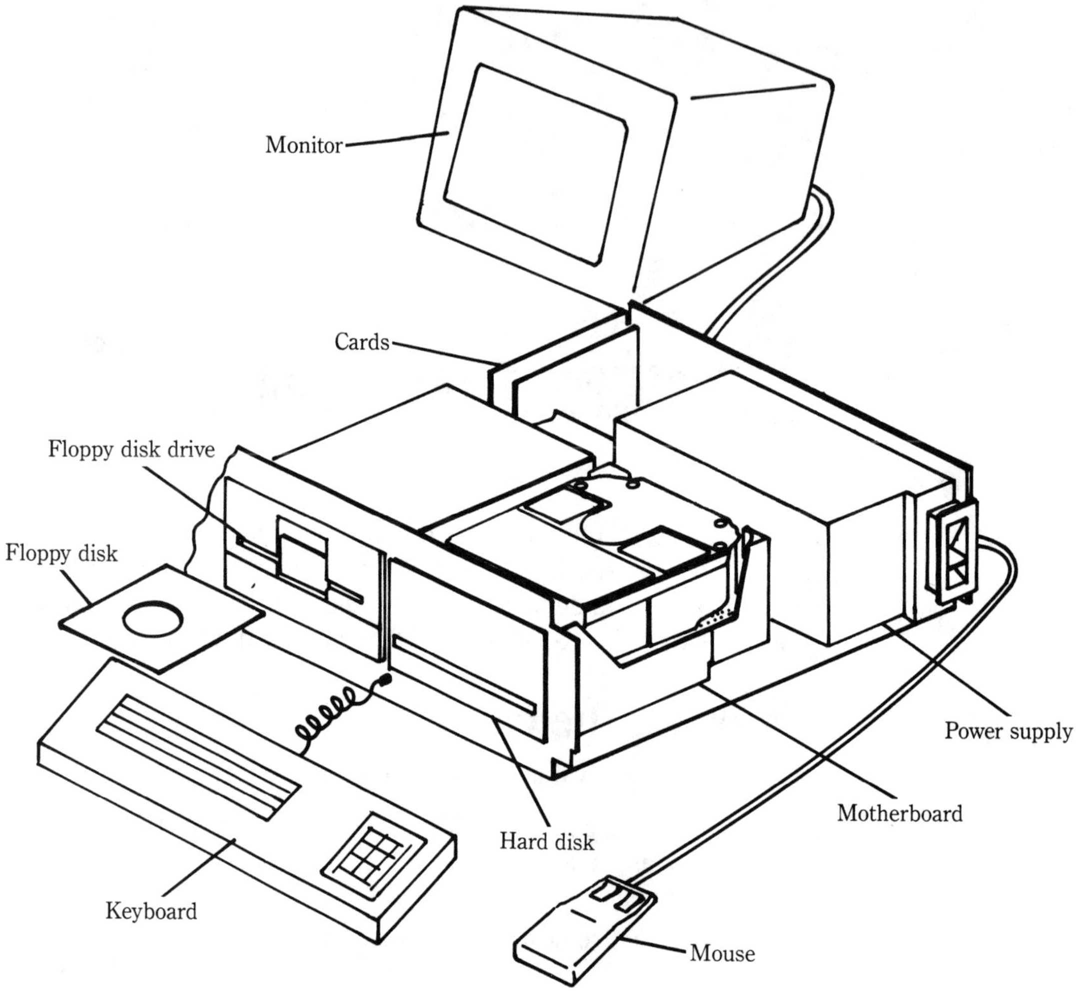


**1-1** Exploded view of PC.

If you have trouble removing the cover, consult your computer installation manual. If at this point you still have trouble, you should seek the assistance of someone with more experience to help you and work with you through the rest of the book.

# Chips and cards

Throughout the text, I refer to computer *chips* and *cards*. For those of you who are unfamiliar with hardware terminology, computer chips are black "bug-like" pieces of plastic that contain thousands of small electronic components (see Fig. 1-2). Cards (also called boards) are con-

**1-2** Various computer chips.

structed of plastic laminates, and hold dozens or even hundreds of chips, as well as other electronic parts such as resistors, capacitors, transistors, and the like (see Fig. 1-3).

Inside the computer on the bottom surface, you can see a number of parallel slotted tracks. These tracks are intended for the insertion of PC cards or boards. Some of these tracks are half the size of the others

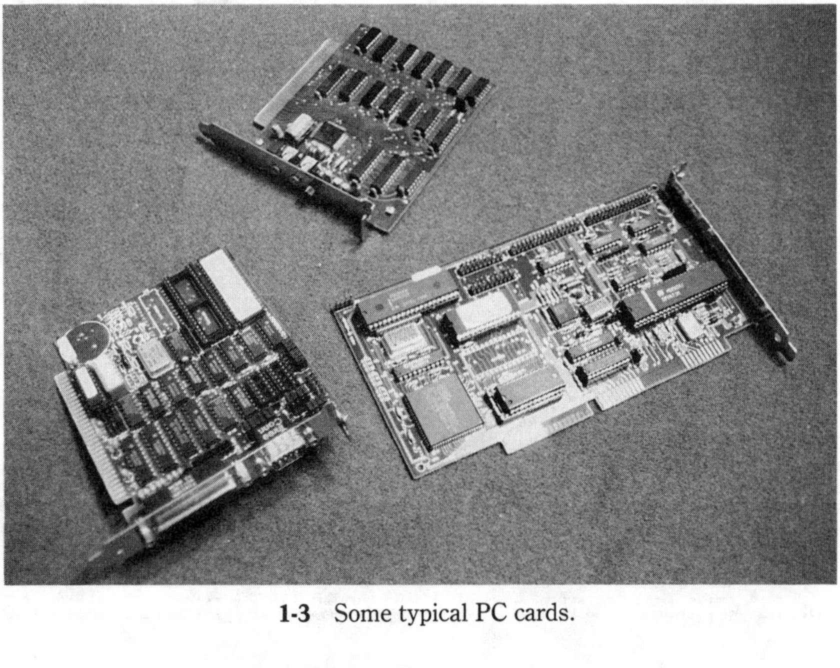

**1-3** Some typical PC cards.

and are designed to accommodate specific cards. The long tracks generally accommodate all cards.

Cards come in two different sizes: *half-size* and *full-size*, the full-size card being twice as long as the half-size card. Half-size cards (also called *half cards*) fit in any slot, full or half. A full-size card might fit into the shorter slot, if its connector is intended for a half-slot, but always fits in a full slot. Figure 1-3 shows some typical PC cards. Note that before you install a card, you must remove the metal slot cover by loosening its screw. Save this screw to secure the card you are installing; the slot cover is no longer needed.

# PC architecture

The general architecture of the IBM PC family of computers (indeed most computers) consists of many components connected to an internal highway of wires called a *bus*. These components are either on or connected to a large flat board inside the computer called the *motherboard*. Figure 1-4 should help you visualize the logical relationship between the parts of the computer and the bus. Later, I discuss each in detail.

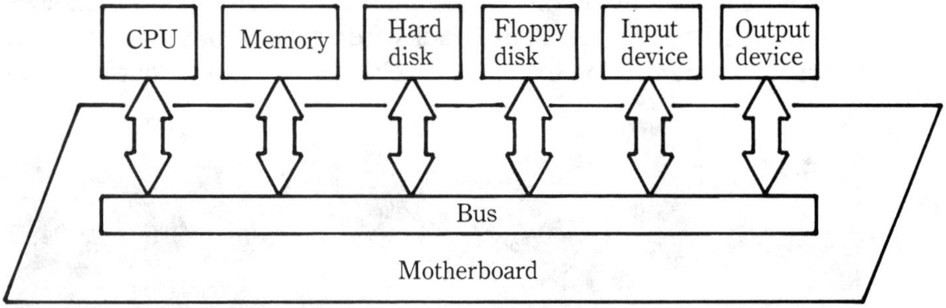


**1-4** Connection of parts to the bus.

# The bus

Within the computer are actually two main busses, an external one for the entire system that traverses the motherboard and other components of the computer, and one that is internal to the microprocessor. The number of "lanes" or wires on these highways, along with other factors, determines whether the computer is an IBM PC, XT, or AT type. (In fact, both the internal and external busses themselves consist of two busses called the *data bus* and *address bus*. The data and address busses will be referred to collectively as *the bus*.) Differences in the external or *system bus* render components that work with one machine incompatible with others.

**NOTE:** There is also a power bus. This bus is used to distribute power amongst the various devices of the computer. The only interaction you will have with this bus is in connecting and disconnecting to it via the power supply.

# Motherboard

When you remove the cover from the computer, you will see the motherboard. This is the large circuit board constructed of laminated plastic that holds many chips and other electronic devices. It is the centerpiece of your computer. The motherboard is securely screwed or bolted in to the computer and should only be removed for replacement or upgrade (see Fig. 1-5). Unfortunately, in some poorly designed computers the motherboard needs to be removed to add a coprocessor, memory, or other devices.

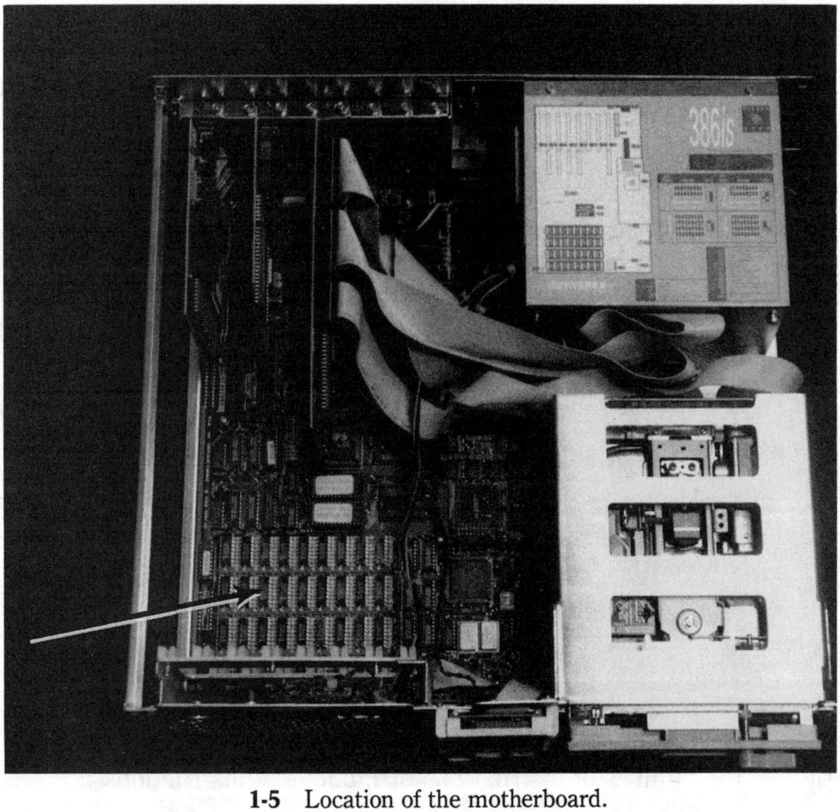


**1-5** Location of the motherboard.

Occasionally a second board called a *daughterboard* is directly attached to the motherboard in order to enhance its performance, for example from an XT class to an AT class computer.

The two other important components of the computer that reside on the motherboard are the BIOS and the clock.

## BIOS chips

The BIOS, which stands for Basic Input/Output System, is a type of ROM memory (see chapter 4) that resides on a group of chips called the BIOS chips. Each set of BIOS chips contains device controllers that typically differ from machine to machine and from one version to the next. Replacing older BIOS versions is an important part of upgrading any PC.

## Clock

On PC, XT, or AT type computers, special software is constantly updating the date and time in some special memory location. On most PC and XT computers, the current date and time is lost when the computer is turned off, and therefore you must reenter them when restarting the computer. However, you can purchase special add-on cards that have a continuous clock. These cards keep track of the date and time even when the computer is off. In this case, you must set up special software routines to run automatically, each time the computer is turned on, to reload the computer with the current date and time from the card. In AT-style computers this feature is built in.

Because the clock is used to keep track of both date and time, it must be updated even when the computer is off. Special batteries provide the power to do this, and also continuously store information about the computer configuration. When the batteries die, very strange problems can occur.

**NOTE:** During the transfer of data from disks to memory, the clock is temporarily disabled, and thus loses time.

Incidentally it is said that the year 2000 will cause problems for many older computer programs because they were not written to handle dates past 1999.

A second kind of clock is independent of the time-keeping one and is found on all microcomputers. This clock, sometimes called the *system clock*, provides timing and synchronization for various functions occurring within the microprocessor, and with other devices. Naturally, the faster the system clock rate, the faster the CPU *throughput*; that is, the number of instructions or millions of instructions per second (MIPS) that can be performed. Slow PCs have clock rates of less than four million cycles per second (megahertz or MHz) while fast ATs have system clock rates in excess of 33 MHz. Note that the allowable system clock rate is determined by a variety of factors such as the switching speeds of various components in the system, so that typically the clock cannot just be "cranked up" to increase performance. Table 1-1 gives the standard clock rates for various microcomputers. "Turbo" versions of these computers have significantly faster clock rates and thus higher throughput.

**Table 1-1. Common clock rates.**

| Model | Clock rate (MHz) |
|---|---|
| PC | 4.77 |
| XT | 4.77 |
| AT (80286) | 6/8 |
| AT | 16/20/25/33 |

Besides differences in architecture, microprocessors can differ in system clock speed. For example, the 80286 chip has siblings running at 8 MHz, 16 MHz, 20 MHz, 25 MHz and more, each corresponding to a faster microprocessor with resultant higher performance.

# Microprocessor and coprocessor

The heart of the PC or any computer is the *central processing unit* or CPU. For microcomputers, the CPU resides on a single chip called a microcprocessor chip or *microprocessor* for short. A sample microprocessor is shown in Fig. 1-6.

Microprocessors differ substantially based on the number of *registers* (special internal memory locations), internal bus width, and on the basic computation functions that can be performed called the *instruction set*. However, I am primarily interested in the Intel 8086 and 80X86 family of microprocessors. These are the Intel 8088, 8086, 80286, 80386, 80386sx, and 80486. I will discuss briefly the differences between these microprocessors shortly.

To enhance the speed of certain operations a second independent microprocessor, called a *coprocessor*, is sometimes added to the computer. The coprocessor usually can perform *floating point* (operations on decimal numbers) and other mathematical operations faster than the main microprocessor, so that the effective throughput of the system is increased. The Intel numbers for coprocessors track those for

**1-6** Intel 80286/sx microprocessor.

the main processors; that is, for the Intel processors mentioned above the corresponding coprocessors are the 8087, 80287, 80387, 80387sx and 80487 (see chapter 3).

# Memory

Electronic computer memory is composed of many millions of binary digits. The binary digit, called a *bit*, is the most fundamental unit of storage. A bit of memory is like a switch that can be either *on* or *off*; that is, it can contain either a "1" or a "0." Bits are further organized into groups of eight called *bytes*. (Some people call groups of four bits *nibbles*.) Bits are further grouped into units called *words*. The size of the word, however, depends on the size of the internal bus. For example, an AT with a 32-bit internal bus has 32-bit words, while an XT has 16-bit words.

Main memory can be divided into two types, *static* and *dynamic*. Dynamic memory uses a stored capacitive charge to represent the one or zero value in the memory cell. Since capacitors leak their charge slowly they must be refreshed periodically or dynamically. Static RAMs store their charge in a way the does not require refresh. Dynamic RAM requires less power and so is ideal for use with laptop computers that use batteries for a power supply.

The way that information such as large numbers, characters, or names can be stored in the computer is fascinating, but beyond the scope of this book. For now, assume that large whole numbers can be stored in the computer using the *binary expansion* of the number. Fractional numbers are stored using a similar but more complex scheme, and characters are stored by using an 8-bit numeric code called the *ASCII code*. ASCII stands for American Standard Code for Information Interchange. The appendix contains a partial ASCII table for your reference.

Because the computer deals only in bits, bytes, and words, many associated concepts employ powers of two. That is, recall that

$$2^0 = 1$$

and

$$2^n = \underbrace{2 \bullet 2 \bullet\bullet\bullet 2}_{n \text{ times}}$$

Other powers of 2 are given in Table 1-2.

**Table 1-2. Powers of 2.**

| Power of 2 | Value | Power of 2 | Value | Power of 2 | Value |
|---|---|---|---|---|---|
| $2^1$ | 2 | $2^9$ | 512 | $2^{17}$ | 131,072 |
| $2^2$ | 4 | $2^{10}$ | 1,024 | $2^{18}$ | 262,144 |
| $2^3$ | 8 | $2^{11}$ | 2,048 | $2^{19}$ | 524,288 |
| $2^4$ | 16 | $2^{12}$ | 4,096 | $2^{20}$ | 1,048,576 |
| $2^5$ | 32 | $2^{13}$ | 8,192 | $2^{21}$ | 2,097,152 |
| $2^6$ | 64 | $2^{14}$ | 16,384 | $2^{22}$ | 4,194,304 |
| $2^7$ | 128 | $2^{15}$ | 32,768 | $2^{23}$ | 8,388,608 |
| $2^8$ | 256 | $2^{16}$ | 65,536 | $2^{24}$ | 16,777,216 |

By convention we call the number 1024 "one k" (for kilo) or "1K" so that the number 4096 is called 4K and the number 65536 is called 64K and so on. Thus when we refer to 256K we mean 1024•256 = 262,144 kilobytes. If we refer to "mega" or "1M" of something we mean 1024•1024 = 1,048,576 or roughly 1 million of that something. Thus 1 megabyte or Mb represents about 1 million bytes. Table 1-3 contains a list of values of some powers of 2 and their conventional names.

Incidentally, I use a variety of strange-sounding prefixes throughout the text. Table 1-4 contains a list of these for your reference.

Memory is usually separated into two categories: *read only memory* (ROM) and read/write memory or *random access memory* (RAM). ROM

**Table 1-3. Conventional names of some numeric values.**

| Value | Conventional name | Value | Conventional name |
|---|---|---|---|
| 1,024 | 1K | 262,144 | 256K |
| 2,048 | 2K | 524,288 | 512K |
| 4,096 | 4K | 1,048,576 | 1M |
| 8,192 | 8K | 2,097,152 | 2M |
| 16,384 | 16K | 4,194,304 | 4M |
| 32,768 | 32K | 8,388,608 | 8M |
| 65,536 | 64K | 16,777,216 | 16M |
| 131,072 | 128K | | |

**Table 1-4. Commonly used prefixes.**

| Number | Numerical value | Abbreviation |
|---|---|---|
| 0.000000000000001 | — | femto |
| 0.000000000001 | trillionths | pico |
| 0.000000001 | billionths | nano |
| 0.000001 | millionths | micro |
| 0.001 | thousandths | milli |
| 1,000 | thousands | kilo |
| 1,000,000 | millions | mega |
| 1,000,000,000 | billions | giga |
| 1,000,000,000,000 | trillions | terra |

typically contains programs written by the computer manufacturer, while RAM is used by the programs you will be running and creating.

The amount of memory the system can utilize is dictated by the architecture of the microprocessor. I discuss this further in chapter 4.

# Mass storage devices

The ability to store large amounts of data is a chief feature of a computer system. Most PCs have two main methods for storage of data: hard disks and floppy disks.

## Hard disk

A hard disk is essential for the permanent storage of large amounts of data, and many programs will not run without one. Hard disks come in various capacities from as small as 10Mb to 300Mb and larger (see Fig. 1-7). Hard disk drive technologies vary greatly, affecting both the amount of information that can be stored and the *access time* (the amount of time it takes for data requested from the disk to become available).

**1-7** A typical 80Mb hard disk drive.

The first hard drive in the system is referred to by DOS as drive C, while subsequent drives are referred to as D, E, and so forth. It is important to note the distinction between a *physical* hard disk and a *logical* drive or drives. A single physical hard disk can be divided into several logical drives; that is, drives which are *partitions* of the same hard disk, but which DOS treats as if they were separate. A physical disk is the disk as seen from the human point of view; logical drives represent how the disk is "seen" or treated by the operating system. Thus, a single computer system may have one or more physical hard disks, each of which is divided into one or more logical drives. Each logical drive is designated by a single letter such as C, D, E, and so on.

## Floppy disk

At least one floppy disk drive is included with every PC system. However, some systems only support certain low-capacity (360K) drives, while others support the larger capacity (1.2Mb) drives. A sample 1.2Mb floppy disk drive is shown in Fig. 1-8.

Additionally, smaller hard diskettes (sometimes called *microcassettes*) are available. These can store either 720K or 1.44Mb of data. Although these diskettes are becoming more popular, microcassettes are much more expensive than floppy diskettes, and usually only the

**1-8** A typical 1.2Mb floppy disk drive.

AT computer will support a microcassette drive. Chapter 8 contains more information on floppy drive types and their installation.

**Booting from floppy disks** The process of turning on the computer and subsequently starting its main program is called *booting*. A disk (either hard or floppy) that contains enough information to be booted is called a bootable disk or *system disk*. The computer can be booted by turning it on (*cold boot*) or by pressing the reset button, if it exists, or pressing the Ctrl, Alt and Del keys simultaneously (*warm boot*).

The first floppy drive to be installed in the system is denoted drive A by DOS; the second drive is usually denoted drive B. When the system is booted, the floppy drive comes up as drive A (if no bootable hard disk is installed). After that, drives A and B are interchangeable logically. This permits copy operations using a single drive by swapping disks.

# Controller cards

On each computer system, either integrated directly into the motherboard or residing as separate boards, are devices that are used to transfer information between the hard and floppy disks and the computer. These devices are called *controllers* (see Fig. 1-9).

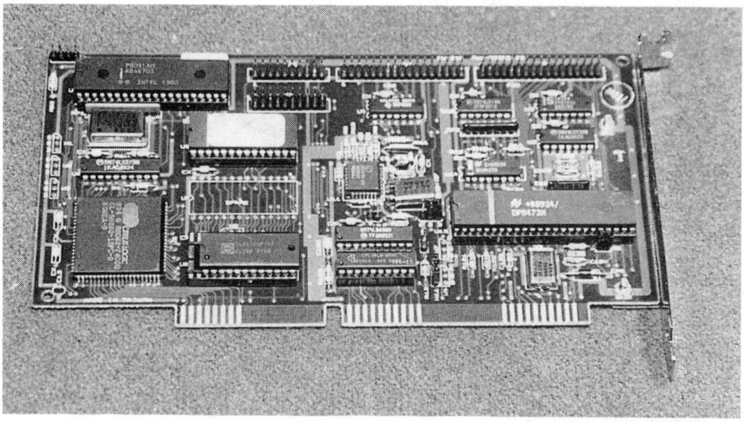

**1-9** A typical combination hard/floppy disk controller card.

Through the controller, the transfer of data takes place between the disk device and CPU. Transfers without the intervention of the CPU are called *direct memory access (DMA)* transfers.

In older PCs and some XTs, the floppy and hard disk controllers were separate, full-size cards. On newer XTs and ATs, the hard and floppy controllers are combined onto one controller card or built directly into the motherboard. You should be aware that there are several different controller and disk technologies that are not compatible. I discuss this further in chapter 7.

# Input/output device

A variety of devices are used to input information into and get information out of the computer. These devices are collectively called *peripherals* or *I/O devices*.

Certain input and output devices are attached to the computer by connecting into cards, while others are attached directly to the motherboard. There are two common types of peripherals supported in this way. One uses a 25-pin D-type connector called a parallel connection, and the other a 9- or 25-pin D-type serial connection (see Fig. 1-10). The parallel connection is usually associated with a device like a printer. On the printer a type of connector called a *Centronics* connector is used. Thus printer cables typically have a male 25-pin D-type connector on one end and a male Centronics connector on the other (see Fig. 1-11). I discuss cables more thoroughly in chapter 12.

Serial connections are usually reserved for devices like modems, mice, plotters, and older printers.

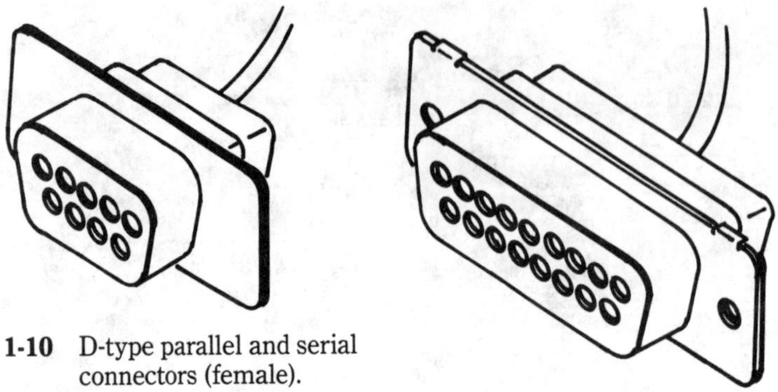

**1-10** D-type parallel and serial connectors (female).

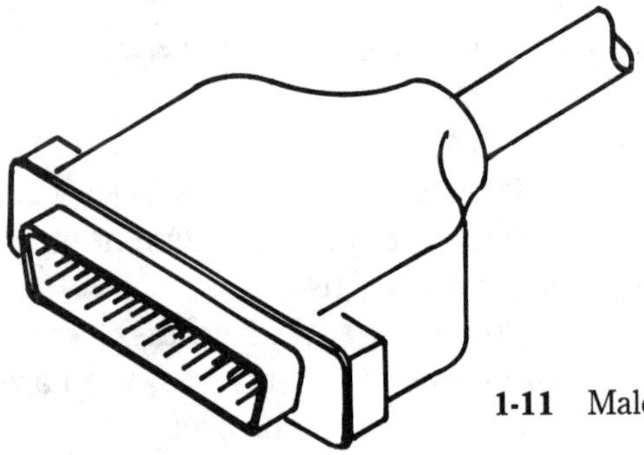

**1-11** Male Centronics connector.

Devices using a parallel connection can transmit or receive one byte (8 bits) at a time, while devices using serial connections can only transmit or receive one bit at a time. Thus, parallel devices usually operate faster than serial ones.

Serial and parallel connections are by no means automatically included with the computer system, especially in XT and PC systems. The PC and XT usually include the parallel connection on the monochrome adapter card, while serial I/O is provided on a single expansion card. When a PC or XT has a color graphics display, the parallel connection is omitted from the graphics adapter and included on an expansion card.

In many AT systems, serial and/or parallel connections are incorporated in the motherboard. Some vendors provide several features on a single card, such as serial and/or parallel connection, clock/calendar, and additional memory. Such a card is called a *multifunction* card.

## Keyboard

A familiar type of input device is the keyboard. The keyboard connects directly into the motherboard via a curly cable and is used to input data in the form of keystrokes.

**1-12** An AT style 101-key keyboard.

Keyboards typically come in two varieties, an 87-key PC-style for the original PC and XT computers, and an AT-style or 101-key for AT computers and compatibles (see Fig. 1-12). Many keyboards have a small switch on the underside that allows you to change from XT to AT style and vice versa.

## Monitor

The visual display or output device of the computer is called a *monitor*, screen, or visual display unit (VDU). Monitors come in a variety of single-color or *monochrome* styles such as white, green, cyan, amber, and so on, and in many color varieties, including EGA, VGA, and so on, that differ in picture resolution or sharpness. I discuss monitors in detail in chapter 9.

## Video cards

The *video card* or *display adapter* is a special board that interfaces the computer monitor to the computer (see Fig. 1-13). Many variations of video cards exist, each with differing capabilities. It is important to understand their differences. Chapter 9 also covers video cards.

## Other peripherals

The variety of input/output devices available commercially has grown from the usual printers and plotters to more exotic devices like FAX boards and optical scanners. Detailed coverage of such devices is

**1-13** A typical video card.

beyond the scope of this book. However, installation of generic input/output devices is covered in chapter 10.

# Power supply

The *power supply* is required to convert the current supplied from your home wall receptable into a form that is usable by the computer. This process involves converting the sinusoidal wave (ac) provided by the home wall receptacle into a direct current (dc) form (see Fig. 1-14). The power supply is typically a square metal box located in the back right hand corner of the computer (it's about the size of four stacked paperback books) and the computer's on/off switch is usually attached directly to it.

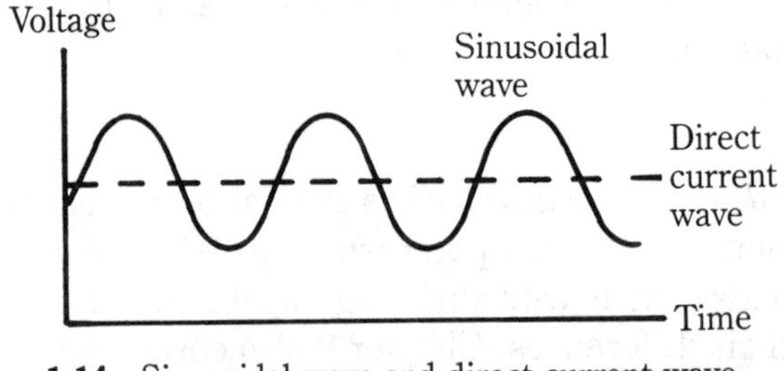


**1-14** Sinusoidal wave and direct current wave.

The capability of your power supply dictates the number of devices that can be added to your system. Selection and installation of power supplies is discussed in chapter 11.

# Operating system

Although I have been talking mostly about hardware—the physical parts of the computer—in this section, I should mention briefly the instructions that control the computer, called the *software*. Software is traditionally divided into two categories: *system programs* and *application programs*. System programs include all the software that interfaces with the underlying computer hardware, such as the BIOS routines, the command interpreter, and other device-controlling software. Application programs are programs that users write to solve specific problems such as payroll preparation, inventory, and so forth.

An *operating system* is a collection of software that facilitates the use of the underlying hardware and manages the resources of the computer. It is a specialized collection of system programs that work together in the same way regardless of which computer they are on. It is through deliberate effort that the commands and functions provided by a specific operating system like DOS are the same from computer to computer.

DOS stands for *disk operating system*. There are several versions of DOS, each with varying capabilities, and it is important that you be aware of these. I cover some of these points in chapter 13.

# Chapter 2

# Basic concepts of repair

This chapter is concerned with the basic practices of computer repair and maintenance. These practices are implied throughout the text and should be followed at all times unless otherwise indicated.

## Backup first

Before any serious repairs or modifications are to be done, indeed on some regular schedule, your computer's hard disk contents should be backed up to floppy disks (or to a tape backup unit if available).

Tape backup units are special devices that are connected directly to the floppy disk controller, and can store many megabytes of information on a cassette-like cartridge. Installation of tape backup units is manufacturer dependent but in many cases is similar to the installation of a floppy disk drive (see chapter 8). Some tape units, however, require a separate controller card.

DOS versions prior to 4.0 provide backup and restore utilities that are difficult to use (see chapter 14). Several commercial software tools for backing up your system are available and some of them are discussed in chapter 14. If only a few critical files need to be backed up, you can consider using a simple DOS copy command or build a *batch file* (a series of DOS commands) which contains the appropriate commands. In all cases you should label your backup disks in order and date them. Never use a single set of backup disks because if a problem (e.g., a power outage) occurs during backup, not only will your hard disk be ruined but so will your only set of backups. Thus, it is desirable to use two sets of backup disks and rotate them. In addition, you should keep a hard copy listing of the directory contents of all backup disks for easy reference.

# Power off

At all times, unless otherwise explicitly directed or when running software, the computer must be OFF and the power cord should be unplugged to prevent electric shock and to protect your computer. You should always wait a few minutes after you unplug the computer before you open it.

WARNING! *To prevent electric shock and damage to the computer, the computer must be* OFF *and* UNPLUGGED *from the wall socket when replacing or servicing any hardware in the system.*

WARNING! *After unplugging the computer, wait a few minutes before working on it. Large capacitors around the power supply can store a significant charge for several minutes—enough to give you quite a zap!*

# Replace one thing at a time

When troubleshooting a computer or when adding new components, it is wise to add or change only one component at a time. This may seem like additional effort, but if something goes wrong you will immediately be able to determine what caused the problem. If you change several components simultaneously and there is a problem—which one caused it? Doctors use a similar technique to determine food allergies by having a patient fast and then adding foods to the diet one by one.

# Testing

At each phase of repair or modification, you should test each change thoroughly before moving on to the next phase. This method ensures that each part of the overall repair is correct and cannot affect future changes to the system.

Upon initial setup of your computer (or after making changes), you should perform a *burn-in*; that is, let the computer run overnight to flush out major problems quickly. Although computer manufacturers usually do this prior to delivery, it is a good idea to do it again. It turns out that in hardware components most errors occur either very early or very late in the life of the component. The so-called *bathtub curve* (Fig. 2-1) describes this effect. The purpose of burn-in testing is to get past the leftmost part of the bathtub curve quickly.

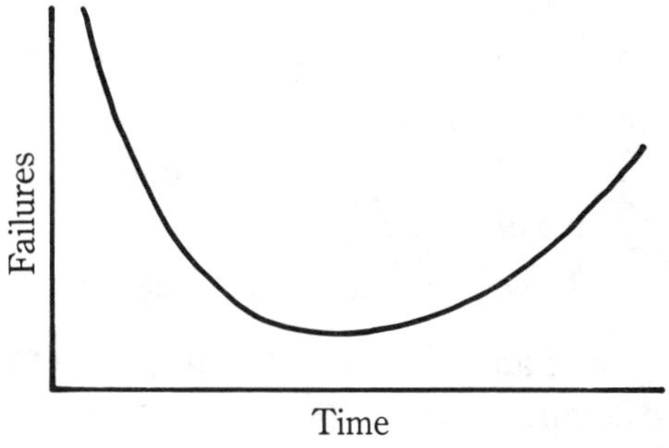


**2-1** The bathtub reliability curve.

# Setup programs

Most computers of the AT class and some of the PC and XT class store system configuration parameters in battery backed-up memory. These parameters must be reset when changing hardware and in cases when the battery runs low. Often power surges due to storms or power fluctuations can alter the system configuration parameters.

Special programs called *setup programs* are provided with such computers to set or reset the system configuration parameters. These programs are usually stored on the "utilities disk" or are part of the BIOS, and are entered by pressing a special key during booting (check your manual). Some machines will automatically enter the setup program when a mismatch between installed hardware and the set parameters is detected.

You must run the setup program each time you change or replace a particular hardware component, and I will remind you of this.

**NOTE:** On older XTs and PCs there is no setup procedure. Instead, you set hardware switches on the motherboard. See chapter 13 and your computer's installation manual for more information on this.

# Dust and dirt

Dust and dirt can harm many of the components of your computer. A clogged fan can cause the computer to overheat, but this is not the worst of your worries—dust particles can destroy your hard or floppy disks and short circuit computer chips. Dust inside the keyboard can also stick or disable keys. To moderate this problem, one should keep the computer environment as dust free as possible. The following suggestions will help you.

- Do not smoke around the computer.
- Use ionizing air filters to remove dust from the air.
- Avoid the use of antistatic dusts on carpets.
- Carefully vacuum your computer keyboard, fan area, and front panel regularly.
- Avoid the temptation to eat or drink around the computer.

Dust and dirt can be removed from the motherboard by opening the computer (power off!) and carefully vacuuming inside. You can also wipe all electronic parts with a gauze pad lightly soaked with an isopropyl alcohol solvent—the kind used to clean records is fine. To remove dust from the floppy drive, manufacturers sell a mild abrasive disk soaked in alcohol that is placed in the drive and rotated briefly.

# Basic disaster prevention

Your computer system represents a large investment in money, time and valuable data. In order to prevent damage to the system and loss of critical data it is very important to follow these guidelines:

- Never turn off the computer while an application program is running.
- If power is in danger of being interrupted (e.g., during a violent thunder storm), do not use the computer and make sure it is unplugged.
- Keep liquids and food away from the system—spills can be a disaster.
- Back up critical data on a daily, weekly, or monthly basis.
- If your computer does not have an autopark feature, be sure to run a park program before you turn off the computer. (See chapter 7.)
- Keep the system covered when not in use to prevent collection of dust.
- Use a surge protector or UPS. (See next section and chapter 11.)

# Regular maintenance

Some basic preventive maintenance can preserve your computer and save you from serious problems in the long run. In addition to turning off the computer during electrical storms and power fluctuations, investment in a decent *surge protector* is a wise decision. For those of you with electronics knowledge, simple surge protectors use a zener diode in parallel to the mainline power to filter high-voltage spikes plus a series capacitor to filter high-frequency noise. Although better computers have some kind of surge protection built in, additional protection is advisable.

Turning off the screen or turning down the brightness during long periods of inactivity prevents a burned-in image from appearing on your screens. You can also purchase utility programs which blank the screen after a period of inactivity.

Regular maintenance enhances your system's long-term performance. The following tasks should be performed monthly or semimonthly:

1. Clean the floppy disk drive heads.
2. Delete all unnecessary files.
3. Perform a hard disk CHKDSK.
4. Back up the hard disk unit completely.
5. Vacuum or blow any dust away from the fan area.
6. Vacuum or blow all dust from the keyboard.
7. Check and secure all cable connections.
8. Compress hard disk.

Items 1, 3, 5 and 7 are discussed in chapter 8, chapter 7, chapter 5, and chapter 12 respectively. The other items are self-explanatory.

# Hardware basics

In this section I introduce some basic electronic components and the rules for handling them. Those of you who are familiar with these items might want to skip ahead.

## DIP switches

Often when preparing certain components for installation you are required to set certain DIP (Dual In-line Package) switches. These are an array of rocker or slider type switches (see Fig. 2-2). The position of the slider or rocker (up or down) indicates a one or zero. The sense of

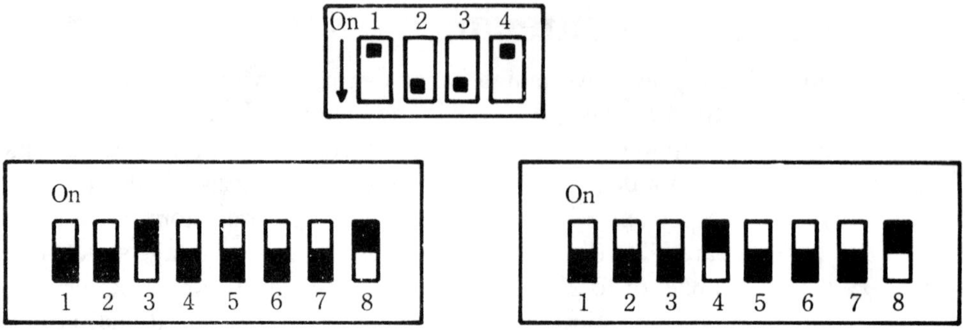


**2-2** DIP switches.

the logic is indicated on the DIP switch itself. The switches are small so they are moved using the point of a pen (don't use a pencil because the lead can break off and cause problems). In addition, the switches must be moved fully up or down (positioning the switch in between is no good). Each switch or combination of switches configures the hardware in a specific manner. For example, DIP switches can be set to indicate how much memory is in your computer or which video card it uses. Most cards that you install yourself also have DIP switches that need to be set.

## Jumper switches

Jumper switches are small plastic clips with conductive material inside that allow a circuit to be completed between two pins of a hardware device. Removing the jumper opens the circuit while installing it closes the circuit. This action has some meaning for the particular device. For example, on a hard disk, a jumper switch is usually used to indicate the device number (e.g., device 0, 1, 2, etc.). Unless you have small fingers, I suggest you use tweezers or needlenose pliers when adding or removing a jumper (see Fig. 2-3).

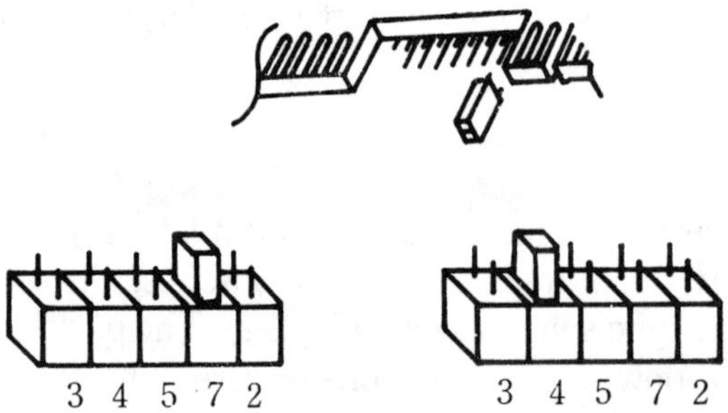


**2-3** Jumper switches.

**NOTE:** Rather than actually removing a jumper switch, you can leave it on one of the two prongs it normally connects to. In this way, no actual connection is made (as if the jumper were removed) but you won't lose the jumper.

## Handling chips and cards

The chips and cards of your computer are very susceptible to damage from electrostatic discharge (ESD)—the static shock you get when walking on carpets too long. For this reason, they are stored in special protective packaging. Before handling any chips or cards you *must discharge yourself*. This can be accomplished by touching the metal chassis of the computer. Special bracelets or *grounding straps*, which connect a part of your body to the computer chassis at all times, can be purchased at any electronics store. These prevent a buildup of static charge when you work on a system for a long time. To summarize, the following tips will prevent accidental ESD:

1. Before touching any chip or card, discharge yourself by touching a metal part of the computer chassis.
2. Wear a grounding strap if possible.
3. Keep chips and cards in their antistatic packaging until you are about to insert them.

## Inserting chips and cards

You will occasionally insert chips such as numeric coprocessor or memory chips into your computer, as well as cards for internal modems, facsimile boards, and so on. This section outlines some general procedures for installation of chips and cards.

**Chips** When inserting a chip into its socket, it is crucial to align it correctly with the receptacle (sometimes called a *carrier*) on the motherboard or card (see Fig. 2-4). Pin 1 of all chips is marked either with a paint dot, an arrow, or a notch. Similarly, the chip holder is also marked at pin 1. You must align the chip with the chip carrier so that pin 1 goes in the right place. Failure to do so can result in *serious damage* to the chip, the computer, or both. In order to align the other pins

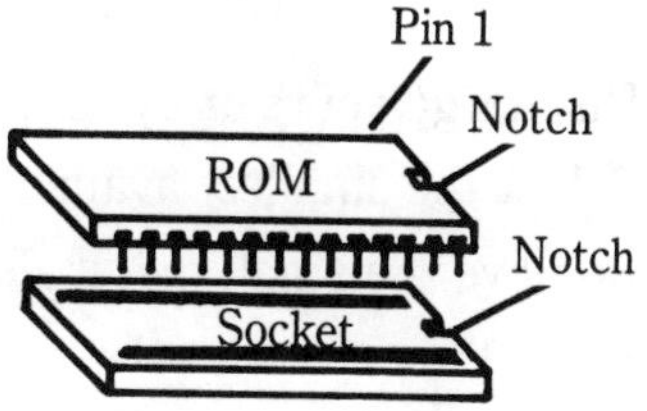


**2-4** Correct chip installation.

with the holes in the chip carrier, you might have to bend them in gently. After inserting each pin, inspect it carefully.

**NOTE:** The pins on the chips are malleable. Bending them three or more times will usually break them off.

Once the chip is properly aligned with the chip carrier, slowly press it into place until the chip is flush with the surface of the chip carrier. Watch out for pins that curl under the chip but do not go into the holes of the chip carrier. If the curl is under the chip it will be difficult to spot and can cause all kinds of problems. If you suspect such a problem, gently pry the chip out with a screwdriver (special chip extractors can also be purchased) and uncurl the offending pin. It is crucial that any chips you install make good contact with the chip carrier. In summary, the steps for inserting a chip are:

1. Discharge yourself by touching the computer chassis.
2. Align chip with carrier.
3. Carefully press chip into place. Be sure it is completely inserted on all sides.
4. Check for curled or bent pins.

**Cards** As I mentioned before, there are two types of cards, full-size cards and half-size cards. Short cards will fit either into the 8-bit (half) slot or the 16-bit (full) slot, but it is best to use the 8-bit slot if available. Full-size cards may be designed to fit into the 8-bit or 16-bit slot, depending on the type of card. Again, use the 8-bit slots whenever possible before using the 16-bit slots.

Select the slot and remove its metal slot cover by removing the screw. The card is then inserted by placing the foil part into an open slot of the motherboard (discharge yourself first). The card must "click in" to the motherboard to ensure good contact. If any of the copper foil shows above the motherboard, then the card is not properly seated. Always be sure to screw the card into the chassis (using the screw from the slot cover) to ensure continued contact. Cards that are badly seated due to poor installation or excessive handling will cause problems. Figure 2-5 depicts the proper card installation technique. To summarize, the steps involved in installing a card into the motherboard are:

1. Discharge yourself by touching the computer chassis.
2. Select the smallest available slot.
3. Remove the small metal slot cover, retaining the screw.
4. Align the card with the slot.

5. Gently press the card in until it is fully inserted. Use a gentle rocking motion if it resists, but never force it.
6. Secure the card with the screw removed from the slot cover.

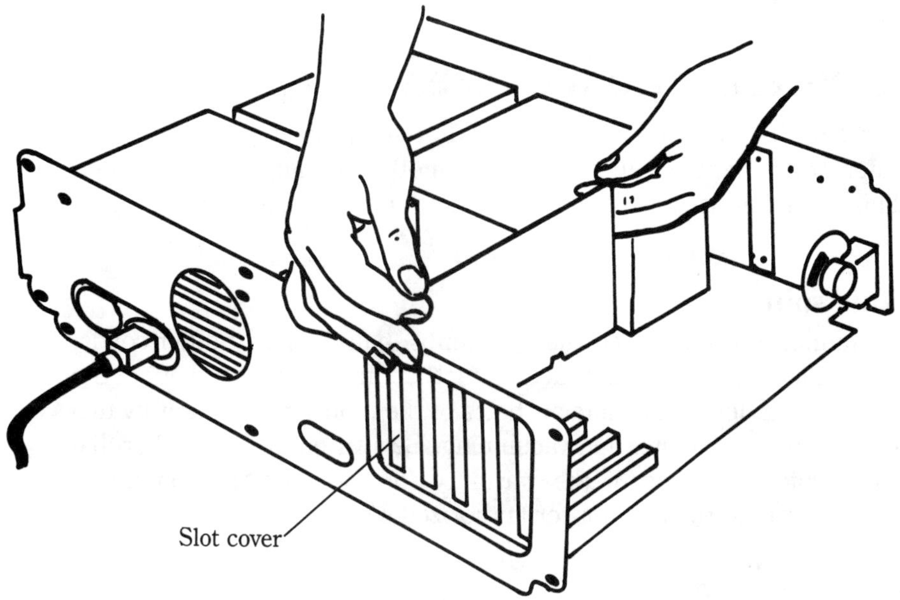


**2-5** Correct card installation.

## A word about soldering

Some of the electronics components in your computer are actually welded or soldered in place. These can be removed with a special tool called a soldering iron, which melts the weld joint and allows for removal of the part. Don't do it. None of the components that you will be replacing need soldering. Those components that do, you won't replace. Any repairs which require this level of effort should probably be done by a professional.

## Tools you will need

The home computer repair technician should have the following ordinary tools in his/her repair kit:

- screwdrivers (various sizes of Phillips and flathead)
- isopropyl alcohol (available at any pharmacy)
- wiping cloths (lint-free cloth)
- needlenose pliers

- grounding strap (available at an electronics store)
- chip extractor (available at an electronics store)
- cleaning diskette (available at a computer store)
- nut driver (available at any hardware store )
- ballpoint pen (for setting DIP switches)

# Recovering from diasters

Occasionally you will spill some liquid or solid material on your computer. If this happens, immediately turn off and unplug the computer. This will minimize any damage and allow you a chance to clean things up.

## Solid spills

Contamination of the machine by crumbs, hairs, dust or other solids, can be handled by carefully vacuuming them from inside and out of the computer. If debris falls into air holes of the monitor, remove it by disassembling the monitor and vacuuming. Be aware that this will probably violate the terms of the warranty for the monitor. You might consider taking the monitor for authorized service instead.

## Liquid spills

Spills of liquids are especially destructive. Before assessing the damage, unplug the computer and remove the cover. Wipe away as much water as possible with sponges or soft cloths. Allow all components to air dry thoroughly.

Once all components are dry, simply add them back one at a time and determine if any are damaged.

If the computer is violated by any liquid other than water, it can cause problems, even after drying. In this case flush the offending liquid with isopropyl alcohol and allow the machine to dry thoroughly.

## Fire damage

Damage from fire, smoke and water will probably destroy your computer. However, if it appears that the machine has some hope of salvage, you can try cleaning each board with isopropyl alcohol. Any infiltration by water or other materials should be handled as discussed in the above two sections.

# Chapter 3

# Microprocessor and coprocessor

This chapter looks at the installation and troubleshooting of the heart of the computer—the microprocessor and its kin, the coprocessor. I examine the various types of microprocessors as they relate to different microcomputer architectures. In particular, I focus on internal and external data bus sizes and address bus size. The address bus size determines the amount of memory which the system can support, and is discussed in chapter 4. Table 3-1 summarizes the salient features of these discussions. If you are installing or replacing the microprocessor for a system, make sure that you use the correct type.

## PC

The standard IBM PC type computer uses the original Intel 8088 microprocessor with an 8-bit internal and an 8-bit external data bus, which severely limits throughput. Address space is limited to 1Mb by a 20-bit address bus. The PC can also accommodate an external hard disk as an add-on.

## XT

The IBM XT type computers are built around the Intel 8088 architecture (with the exception of the AT&T 6300 which is based on the 8086 chip, and the XT/286, based on the 80286 chip). These also have an

**Table 3-1. Salient features of some Intel microprocessors.**

| Microprocessor | Typical system | Int. data bus | Ext. data bus | Address bus |
|---|---|---|---|---|
| 8088 | PC,XT | 8-bit | 8-bit | 20-bit |
| 8086 | AT&T 6300 | 8-bit | 16-bit | 20-bit |
| 80286 | AT | 16-bit | 16-bit | 24-bit |
| 80386 | AT | 32-bit | 32-bit | 32-bit |
| 80386sx | AT | 32-bit | 16-bit | 24-bit |
| 80486 | AT | 32-bit | 32-bit | 32-bit |

internal data bus size of 8 bits, an external data bus size of 8 bits, and an address bus size of 20 bits. At its introduction the XT had two features which made it superior to the PC: DOS 2.0, and an integral 10Mb hard disk.

The XT has increased performance over the PC primarily due to the increased disk transfer rate of the hard disk and improved operating system features. In addition, the XT can use all plug-in components that conform to the PC's 8-bit system bus size.

# AT

The IBM AT models use the Intel 80286 microprocessor with 16-bit internal and external data bus sizes. Later versions also use the 80386 with 16-bit external and 32-bit internal data bus sizes or the 80486 with 32-bit internal and external data bus sizes. The 80286 and 80386sx have 24-bit address busses while the 80386 and 80486 have 32-bit address busses. The 24-bit address bus results in a possible address space of 16Mb and the 32-bit address bus can support an address space 256 times that.

The system clock rates have increased as well. There is also a less expensive version of the 80386 called the 80386sx that has the same instruction set as the 386, but a different internal architecture and slower clock speed. Subsequently, when we refer to "ATs" we mean the Intel 286-, 386-, 386sx-, and 486-based systems collectively.

# Micro-channel

The IBM micro-channel architecture is specific to the PS/2 model 50 series of personal computers. This text does not deal directly with the service and repair of such machines, but many of the concepts and techniques I discuss are in fact the same.

# Installing or replacing microprocessors

If you have reason to suspect that the microprocessor is faulty (e.g., as reported by the power-on diagnostic) you must remove the old one and replace it. Be sure that the characteristics of the replacement microprocessor are the same as those for the old one; that is, it must have the same part number. This ensures that the bus width, clock speed, and instruction set are the same (see "Upgrading the microprocessor").

Installing or replacing the microprocessor can be relatively simple, so long as the original chip has not been soldered directly into the board. If it has, a simple but delicate desoldering procedure is required. This is not recommended for beginners.

If the chip is not soldered into its holder, gently pry it loose with a screwdriver or similar tool. Place the new chip over the holder so that the notch or dot on the chip matches the notch in the chip holder. Be sure that the legs of the chip align with the holes in the chip holder. Gently push the chip into place—nudge the front and back of the chip gently until the chip sits flush. Do not force the chip. Of course, all of this should occur with the power off and the plug out.

**NOTE:** 80386 and 80387 chips are square in shape with pins all around and underneath. These pins are not malleable. Be careful when extracting this chip with a screwdriver because you might break off some pins. You should probably use a special chip extractor tool to remove this chip.

After installing the chip, turn on the computer and observe the diagnostics to determine if the installation was successful.

**WARNING!** *Failure to line the chip up correctly in its holder pack will result in damage to the chip and/or the computer.*

**WARNING!** *A static discharge from you at this point can destroy the microprocessor chip. Be sure to discharge yourself by touching the metal chassis of the computer before handling the chip.*

To summarize, the following steps are needed to replace the microprocessor chip (if it is not soldered in place):

1. Discharge yourself by touching the computer chassis.
2. Remove the existing microprocessor chip by gently prying it out with a screwdriver.
3. Align the new chip with the carrier.

4. Gently press the chip into place.
5. Plug in the computer, turn on the power, and observe the power-on diagnostics.
6. Run any other manufacturer-supplied diagnostics.

# Upgrading the microprocessor

Typically, upgrading the processor of the computer involves more than just switching chips. The entire architecture of the computer is based on the internal and external bus size of the microprocessor. Thus, changing only the microprocessor can be disastrous. Similarly, revving up the system clock speed will not work because the rest of the system probably cannot accommodate this increase. Thus if you want to upgrade the processor, you must buy a manufacturer's upgrade kit, which typically involves the addition of a daughterboard and the replacement of several chips. Discussion of this upgrade is beyond the scope of this book.

# Numeric coprocessor

Numeric coprocessors speed the execution of certain instructions and effectively extend the instruction set. To install the coprocessor, follow the same procedure used for the microprocessor.

**NOTE:** Make sure you use the correct coprocessor type. For example, the 8088 uses the 8087 coprocessor, while the 80286 uses the 80287. Also, be sure that the clock speed of the coprocessor is closely matched to the main processor (it should be as fast or slower; coprocessors are not manufactured for all the clocks speeds at which the main processors run). Table 3-2 lists several microprocessors and their companion coprocessors. In any case, the best way to prevent timing problems is to acquire the processor and coprocessor together as a kit.

**Table 3-2. Microprocessors and their companion coprocessors.**

| Microprocessor | Coprocessor |
|---|---|
| 8088 | 8087 |
| 8086 | 8087 |
| 80286 | 80287 |
| 80386 | 80387 |
| 80386sx | 80387sx |
| 80486 | 80487 |

Be sure to run setup after installation of the coprocessor to inform the system that it has been installed, and set any DIP or jumper switches required (see your computer's installation manual).

In addition, the software you are using must be set to take advantage of the coprocessor. Often this means either reinstalling software or running its setup program again. Check the documentation for the software package concerned to determine how it can exploit the coprocessor. To summarize, follow these steps to replace or add the numeric coprocessor:

1. Discharge yourself by touching the computer chassis.
2. Remove any existing coprocessor chip by gently prying it out with a screwdriver.
3. Align the new chip with the carrier.
4. Gently press the chip into place.
5. Plug in the computer, turn on the power, and observe the power-on diagnostics.
6. Run any other manufacturer-supplied diagnostics.
7. Reconfigure all software which may use the coprocessor according to the manufacturer's instructions.

# Replacing the motherboard

While it is really beyond the scope of an introductory text to discuss the replacement of the motherboard, the more advanced user might wish to give it a try. Replacement of the motherboard is warranted when replacement of all other devices has failed to correct a problem, or if the microprocessor is not removable from the motherboard, but needs to be replaced. I assume here that you are not upgrading the computer, but are replacing a faulty motherboard with one of exactly the same type.

To replace the motherboard, all cards, disk drives, and the power supply must be removed according to the procedures outlined in chapters 7, 8, and 11. The memory chips might also have to be removed, depending on whether the new motherboard can use the old chips. The old motherboard is removed by loosening any screws or bolts securing it, and the new motherboard is screwed or bolted in its place. After installing the new motherboard, the computer is then reassembled and tested using the manufacturer's diagnostics. To summarize the replacement procedure:

1. Remove all cards, disk drives, and the power supply. (Remove memory chips if needed.)

2. Remove the screws or bolts securing the motherboard.
3. Install the new motherboard in its place.
4. Reinstall the cards, disk drive, and power supply.

# Troubleshooting

The following hints might be helpful when diagnosing problems with the microprocessor or coprocessor.

1. Many manufacturers provide diagnostics on diskette for the microprocessor that can be used to great advantage.
2. Be sure your software is "aware" of a newly installed numeric coprocessor. You might have to reinstall the software or set certain software parameters to indicate the presence of the coprocessor.
3. Do you have two video cards installed in your system? They may not be correctly configured. Such a situation can cause apparent CPU problems.
4. On some systems, the power-on diagnostics may run with just a keyboard connected. In this case, you can unplug every peripheral including disks and monitor, set the DIP switches to indicate the absence of these devices, and power on the computer. If the system beeps, chances are the CPU and motherboard are fine.
5. If after trying the above you conclude that the CPU or motherboard is defective, try replacing the CPU, then the motherboard. This should be your last resort!

# Chapter 4

# Memory

This chapter describes the installation and expansion of system memory or Random Access Memory (RAM).

Most PCs come equipped with only 64K of RAM on the motherboard, while older XTs typically have 256K and the newer ones 640K. ATs sometimes come with a default 512K of memory—inadequate for some applications. Frequently you need to add memory to your system.

## Address space

The *logical address space* of the computer is the maximum computer memory addressable in a fixed word, and is determined by the address bus size. For example, in a PC system with a 20-bit address, there is a possible $2^{20}$ or 1Mb of addressable memory.

Even with 1Mb of logical memory, not all is available for program use. 384K of memory is normally reserved for the BIOS and device controllers (e.g., for the display adapter). This gives PC users an available memory capacity of 640K.

In systems using the 80286 and 80386 chips, the address bus size increases to 24 and 32 bits respectively. This increases the logical address space to 16Mb and 256 times that. However, many application programs and some versions of DOS only support 1Mb of memory.

The *physical address space* is the actual memory on board the system, which can be increased beyond the logical address space using certain hardware schemes. There are two methods for increasing the amount of memory available to the system—expanded memory and extended memory.

# Expanded memory

*Expanded memory* is a technique that allows programs to use the 384K of memory normally reserved for the BIOS and screen memory. In this case 384K of physical memory are added to the system, but special software drivers map the additional memory into the logical address space. The 384K belonging to the BIOS, screen memory, and device controllers are unaffected. See Fig. 4-1.

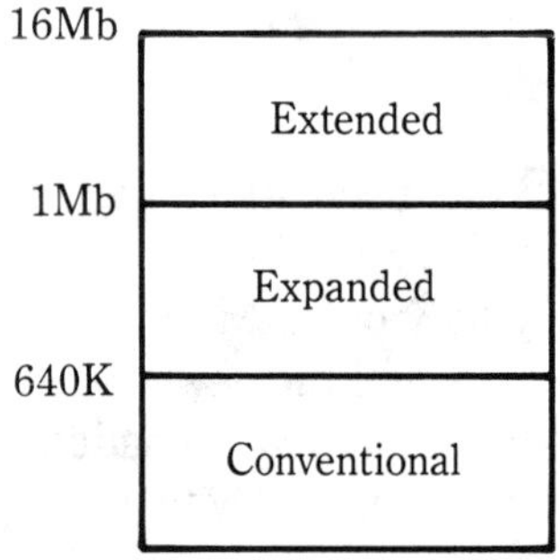


**4-1** A DOS memory map (not to scale).

# Extended memory

Memory that extends beyond the 1Mb logical limit of DOS is called *extended memory*. Typically, extended memory ranges from 1Mb to 16Mb (see Fig. 4-1). Most applications cannot use this area because of the 1Mb address limit of DOS. The DOS vdisk command, however, can be used to create a RAM disk in this area. Also, programs which conform to the Lotus-Intel-Microsoft (LIM) standard and 80X86 processors which run in protected mode can use this region.

**NOTE:** DOS 5.0 takes care of this for you.

# Memory cards

If the motherboard does not accommodate additional memory, then some sort of memory card must be added. Memory expansion cards are usually inexpensive but might be *unpopulated*; that is, no memory chips are on board. You must add the chips yourself. Some multifunction cards also provide space for additional system memory, and can be purchased either populated or unpopulated. If at all possible, purchase fully populated memory cards.

# Memory chips

Memory chips are manufactured by several firms and vary according to quality, price and access times. The *access time* of the chip is the amount of time it takes for data requested from the chip to be placed and ready on the data bus. Access times generally vary from 50 to 100, 120, or 150 nanoseconds (a nanosecond is $1 \times 10^{-9}$ seconds), although there are slower and faster types. The performance of your computer is largely based on the access times of memory, and if you mix memory with different access times, the slowest of the bunch is the speed of your memory.

Chips come in varying sizes (64K, 128K, 256K), but usually come in 1- or 4-bit slices (denoted $\times 1$ and $\times 4$). Thus, to add 64K of memory on an 8-bit bus architecture you will need nine 64K $\times 1$ chips. The ninth chip is for a parity bit that is used during system initialization.

**Example:** On an XT, to add 256K of memory to your system (if the board accommodates 256K chips), you will need nine 256K $\times 1$ chips.

**Example:** The original PC family used 16K chips in 4 banks of 9 chips for a total of 64K or 16 banks of 9 chips for 256K.

More than likely, the XT arrived with 640K of memory that you would like to expand to 1Mb. This requires the addition of 384K of RAM which can be done with nine 256K $\times 1$ chips and nine 128K $\times 1$ chips. Memory chips for ATs usually come in 4-bit slices, but more likely utilize SIMM modules, which are discussed in the next section.

**NOTE:** Chips have become a commodity, so the prices fluctuate wildly. To obtain the best deal you should purchase chips from a reputable mail-order house or computer store.

# SIMM

A new trend in the AT class computers is to use *Serial In-line Memory Modules* or *SIMMs*. A SIMM is a set of memory chips installed on a small PC board (about the size of a couple of postage stamps). The SIMM can be installed quickly by sliding it into its receptacle on the motherboard. SIMMs vary in size and access times but sizes like 256K or 1Mb by 16 bits are common.

# Installing memory

Installing memory on memory cards or directly on the motherboard requires the following four steps:

1. Populate the memory board
2. Set the DIP switches
3. Plug in the board
4. Run setup

If the memory is to be installed directly to the motherboard, then the third step can be skipped.

## Populating the memory board

The first step in *populating* (adding memory chips to) your system board or add-on card is to calculate the number and type of chips necessary to add to your system before purchase. Both the number and type are dictated by the manufacturer, so consult their instruction manual. Appropriate DIP switches are also set, according to manufacturer's instructions.

Physically adding the memory to the motherboard or memory expansion board is simple. Make sure that the correct size (e.g., 64K, 128K, 256K) chip is placed over its socket. Place the new chip over the holder so that the notch or dot on the chip matches the notch in the chip holder. Be sure that the legs of the chip align with the holes in the chip holder. Gently push the chip into place by nudging the front and back of the chip gently until the chip sits flush. Do not force the chip. Continue with the rest of the chips. Of course, all of this should occur with the power off and plug out. The steps to remember here are:

1. Determine correct size and quantity of chips.
2. Follow standard chip installation procedure in chapter 2.

WARNING! *A static discharge from you at this point can destroy the chips. Wear a wrist strap, or be sure to discharge yourself by touching the metal chassis of the computer, before you touch a chip.*

## Setting DIP switches or jumpers

In some systems, especially PCs and XTs, DIP switches or jumpers have to be set on the motherboard to indicate that the new memory has been added. In addition, expansion boards probably need DIP switch settings to indicate how much memory was added. Perform this step according to the manufacturer's instructions.

## Running setup

In AT systems the setup program must be run to indicate that additional memory has been added. If this is not done, a memory parity error failure will occur upon power-on.

After installing the chip, turn on the computer and observe the diagnostics to determine if the installation was successful. A memory count, in kilobytes, will appear in the upper left hand corner of the screen. This number should agree with the total installed memory in your system. Furthermore, if the installation was not successful, some indication such as "memory mismatch" will be displayed.

In some systems a "Parity Check I" error means that a chip on the motherboard is faulty. A "Parity Check II" error indicates an expansion board chip is bad.

## Using chkdsk

Running the DOS chkdsk program also confirms the available main memory. At the DOS prompt type

C>chkdsk

A screen display similar to the following appears:

```
33435648 bytes total disk space
   55296 bytes in 3 hidden files
  124928 bytes in 52 directories
20762624 bytes in 1796 user files
   20480 bytes in bad sectors
12472320 bytes available on disk

  655360 bytes total memory
  594320 bytes free
```

For now, focus only on the last two lines. These indicate the amount of main memory available (total memory) and the amount of memory that is not currently being used by the operating system or other programs (free). See chapter 14 for more details on the chkdsk command.

## Upgrading or replacing memory

As I said before, upgrading the memory by replacing it with chips that have faster access times generally does not improve system performance, as other devices in the system may depend on the memory having a certain speed. You should check your computer's hardware manual before considering such a change.

Replacing a bad memory chip (and they do go bad) is simply a matter of identifying the culprit. However, doing this requires some sophistication. The setup programs for some systems can do this for you, as perhaps can some commercial tools. If you are a capable programmer, you can create your own program that writes various patterns into every memory location and reads them back, but again, this takes skill.

Another method for finding the bad chip is to use a simple *binary search* or divide-and-conquer technique. To do this you use the setup program or DIP switches to reduce the amount of system memory by one-half. If the memory error still occurs, it was in the half that you did not switch. Otherwise, the bad chip was in the half that you disabled. Subsequently disabling one-quarter of the total memory in the half that was deemed bad and then one-eighth, and so on, should eventually lead you to the culprit chip or chips. To summarize, the procedure for identifying a bad chip is:

1. Disable half the memory by setting the appropriate DIP switches or running the setup program.
2. Turn on the computer and observe the power-on diagnostics.
3. If the error is still present, the bad chip is in the enabled half of memory. Otherwise, the bad chip is in the disabled half.
4. Continue from step 1 with the half of memory containing the bad chip. Repeat the procedure until you have isolated the problem.

# BIOS chips

The BIOS, which stands for Basic Input/Output System, is a type of ROM (read only memory) that resides on a group of chips called the BIOS chips. These chips contain some of the operating system. In some systems the contents of the BIOS chips are copied into RAM to enable faster system execution. The area into which the BIOS is copied is called *shadow RAM.*

Each set of BIOS chips contains a set of device controllers that typically differs by machine and operating system version. Replacing older BIOS versions is an important part of upgrading any microcomputer and may be necessary in older computers to support modern disk drives or to eliminate bugs. Damage to the BIOS chips renders the computer useless.

When replacing the BIOS chips, it is crucial that the correct version be used. The BIOS version number and manufacturer can sometimes be determined by watching the screen during power-up, when some systems display the BIOS version number. On systems where this is not true, such as IBM PCs, the BIOS version number may be stamped on the BIOS chips. Similarly, if you see a part number stamped on the chip, you might be able to determine its date of origin by identifying the chip to a knowledgeable sales representative. In any case, before attempting to replace the BIOS be sure to back up the hard disk(s) completely.

The BIOS chips (there are usually three of them) are identified either by a memory map provided by the manufacturer or in the following way. The BIOS chips are often the only chips on the motherboard that are easily removable. To distinguish them from other chips, often they are colored differently; for example, they might be white instead of black. The chips are removed and replaced in the same manner as any other memory chips.

If problems occur after upgrading the BIOS, the hard disk may need to be completely reformatted (low-level, partitioned and DOS—see chapter 7). Also check that all devices such as printers, modems, and so forth, are working normally after the upgrade.

# Troubleshooting

If problems occur with the system memory, consider the following hints.

1. If a parity error occurs, as indicated by the power-up diagnostics, rerun the setup program. Electrical storms can disrupt the physical settings of the computer.
2. If an add-on memory card is being used, try reseating it (remove and reinstall it). A poorly seated memory card is the cause of many mysterious failures.
3. Be sure that any memory chips you have added are properly seated in their holders. Beware of curled pins.
4. Are the chip access times of the newly added memory faster than those of the old chips? They shouldn't be.
5. Check to make sure that the memory chips are all of the correct type.
6. Check the DIP switches and/or rerun setup as required.
7. Sometimes memory error messages are caused by the improper installation of a card.

# Chapter 5

# Keyboard

The keyboard is the user's direct input device to the computer. This chapter considers the maintenance and installation of this device.

There are two main types of keyboards, the PC/XT or 87-key style, and the AT or 101-key style. Most keyboards are interchangeable between computers as long as they are equipped with a switch that makes them compatible with either style.

## Replacement

To remove or replace a keyboard, no special steps are required other than to ensure that the computer is off, and to remove the keyboard cable from its socket either at the rear, front or side of the computer (see Fig. 5-1). When inserting the keyboard cable be sure the plug is in the correct orientation (keyboard plugs are "keyed" so they will only go in one way—the right way). If the keyboard cable is too short for your purposes, extension cables can be purchased.

### AT/XT switch

Many keyboards are designed to work in either PC/XT or AT mode. To select one mode or the other you flip a small switch found either under the keyboard or on the back. The switch should be labeled, and is usually small, so you'll need the point of a pen to flip it. Flip the switch while the power is off.

**5-1** Typical keyboard connection socket.

# Stuck keys

Keys that appear to be stuck or that do not respond when pressed are probably suffering from "dust under the pad." If you gently pry out the key (and underlying mechanism) with a screwdriver, you might expose some circuitry that looks like Fig. 5-2. (Some keyboards are sealed to prevent entry of dust so you won't see this—but neither will you have a problem with dust particles). You may see dust, hair or other garbage fouling this area. Gently vacuum it or blow it away. Replace the mechanism and key—the key won't stick anymore. Flushing the keyboard with alcohol (power off) can often remove foreign particles from under the keypad.

**WARNING!** *On the original IBM PC, the space bar key cannot be removed without breaking it!*

**5-2** Spiral contact under the keypad.

# Cleaning

The surface of the keyboard can be cleaned occasionally either by vacuuming it gently or by blowing it with the vacuum in reverse or with one of the hand held compressed air cans sold in computer stores. Do not clean the keyboard with liquids (except alcohol with the power off). A keyboard cover will prevent accumulation of dust when the computer is not in use.

The following tips are helpful when cleaning the keyboard:

- Use a cloth (paper towels or tissues can break off and leave lint).
- If alcohol is not available, use commercial window cleaners.
- Rub individual keys.

**WARNING!** *Do not drink or eat anything around the keyboard because spills can ruin it!*

# Troubleshooting

The following items should be checked if a problem with the keyboard is suspected.

1. Be sure that the XT/AT switch is set correctly.
2. Be sure that the cable is properly secured to the system unit.
3. Inspect the cable connection from inside the computer. Be sure that the wires attaching the connector to the motherboard are not broken. (If they are they must be resoldered by a professional).

# Chapter 6

# Controller card

The controller card is the electronic interface between a storage device such as a hard or floppy disk and the computer. It is used to transfer information back and forth between the CPU and the disk device. Other devices like tape backup units either have their own controller or can use ordinary floppy disk controllers. This chapter looks at the installation of independent device controllers.

Controller cards come in different varieties; that is, they support different storage methodologies; hard disks only, floppy disks only, or both. For example, old PCs use separate controller cards for the floppy disk and hard disks drives. XT and AT style PCs use separate controller cards or combined half cards that control both floppy and hard disk drives. Most of these combination controllers will support (control) two floppy disk and two hard disk drives. In some systems, and with some disk drive type, the control logic is built directly into the motherboard.

You must not install a noncompatible disk drive with your controller. For example, RLL disk controllers require RLL type disks, and MFM controllers can only support MFM type drives, and so on. Floppy disk drives are the same for all controllers. In this chapter we will look at a variety of disk storage technologies and their controllers.

## Drive types

Current disk/controller technologies differ in price, performance, capacity, and flexibility. I review them here.

## MFM

Modified Frequency Modulation (MFM) is a data-coding scheme used on magnetic recording media such as hard disks. This is a very common storage technology for hard disks under 80Mb.

## RLL

Run Length Limited (RLL) is a data-coding scheme used on magnetic recording media such as disks that compresses data in such a way as to provide 50 percent more storage capacity than MFM. Usually a letter "R" appears in the manufacturer's part number to remind you that the disk is RLL type. The RLL technique is predominantly used with drives for XT computers. Most RLL drives are around 32Mb in size—the limit for most XT systems. RLL, which is now dated, was used to expand the hard disk capabilities of the XT beyond 20Mb.

## SCSI

Small Computer System Interface (SCSI, pronounced "scuzzy"), drives take advantage of a standard interface methodology that is used on a variety of computer types—not just IBM microcomputers and their clones. Many *minicomputers* (small multiuser computers) support "scuzzy" interfaces. SCSI-based systems are easily expandable because the bus interface is standardized. For newer systems, and for drives greater than 80Mb in size, SCSI is the most widely used technology. To install this type of drive you need a SCSI host adapter and mounting kit that can be purchased from the drive manufacturer. Many backup tape drive units use SCSI interfaces.

## ESDI

Enhanced Small Device Interface (ESDI) drives are typically two to four times faster than a standard MFM drive and thus are more suitable for larger disk sizes. Many larger disks (80Mb and above) are ESDI type.

## IDE

Integrated Drive Electronics (IDE), is a relatively new technology that combines the controller card with the hard disk for increased reliability and reduced access times. Although you can purchase separate IDE controllers and drives, this of course defeats the purpose. IDE drives incorporate segment interleaving (see chapter 7) and cache memory for enhanced performance. *Cache memory* is a technique that stores frequently used segments from the disk in fast memory on board the controller.

When you install the IDE drive, you attach a 40-pin cable (plugged directly into the motherboard) to the drive. Physical installation of the drive is the same as for any other drive, as is logical installation.

IDE controllers can be purchased separately from the disk drive and then attached to MFM type disks. These controllers can then support more than one hard disk as well as floppy disks. In this case, the IDE drive is used exactly like an ordinary MFM controller.

# Installation

Installation of the controller card requires no special steps. With the power off, insert the controller card into the smallest slot that will accommodate it. Be sure the controller card is making good contact with the motherboard (see Fig. 6-1). I discuss the cables that connect the controller card to the hard and floppy disk drives in chapters 7 and 8. To summarize, the steps involved in installing a controller card are:

1. Discharge yourself by touching the computer chassis.
2. Select the smallest available slot.
3. Remove the small metal slot cover, retaining the screw.
4. Align the card with the slot.
5. Gently press the card in until it is fully inserted. Use a gentle rocking motion if it resists, but never force it.
6. Secure the card with the screw removed from the slot cover.

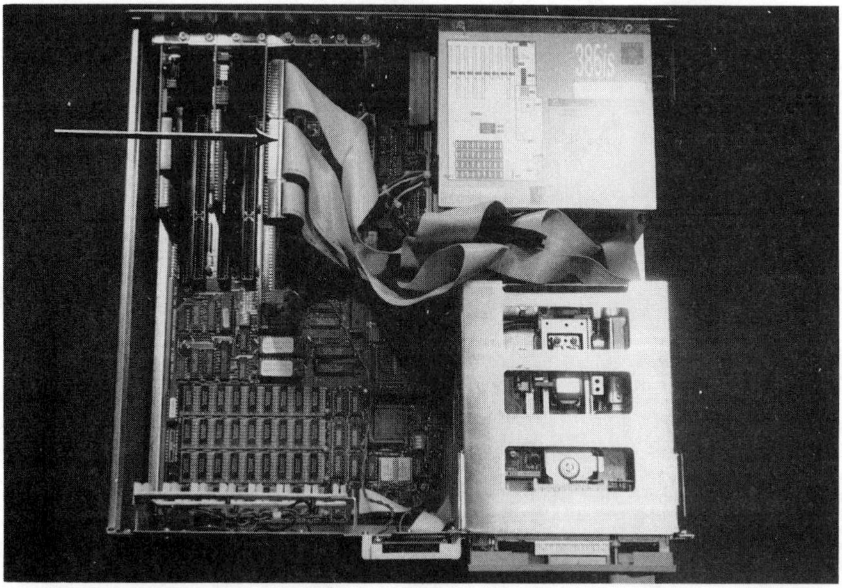


**6-1** Location and installation of controller card.

**NOTE:** In older PCs and XTs the controller card's DMA may conflict with that of tape backup units or LAN (Local Area Network) cards. In this case, the controller is incompatible and must be changed.

# Troubleshooting

The following hints might be helpful when problems with the controller card are suspected:

1. Try reseating the controller card (remove and reinstall it). A poorly seated controller card is the cause of many mysterious failures.
2. Be sure the controller card is compatible with the drive type.
3. Be sure the disk cables are connected correctly and securely to the controller (see chapter 7).
4. Check to see that the disk cables are not cracked or frayed—this can cause problems that appear to be controller-related.
5. Make sure the controller card is not installed in a slot next to the power supply.
6. As a last resort, try moving the controller card to a different slot.

# Chapter 7

# Hard disk drive

The hard disk is the subsystem of the computer that is used for bulk storage of data. Many programs will not run without one. This chapter takes a brief look at how the disks work, and how you can replace, upgrade, and troubleshoot them.

I provide installation instructions only for MFM/RLL disks; however, the installation procedures for other drive types such as IDE, SCSI, and ESDI differ only in how the physical connections are made—typically they use one instead of two cables. The physical installation procedures for these devices are provided by the manufacturer.

## Basic concepts

The hard disk is actually composed of several record-like *platters* sealed in a sturdy case. The number of platters depends on the actual technology of the disk and the amount of data that it needs to store. The platters are metallic, and contain millions of small magnets called *magnetic domains*. These domains are oriented in one of two directions to represent binary 0s and 1s. (In main memory the presence or absence of an electric charge is used to represent 0s or 1s.) For physical reasons, hard disks do not have an infinite useful life. Figure 7-1 gives a block diagram of a typical hard disk.

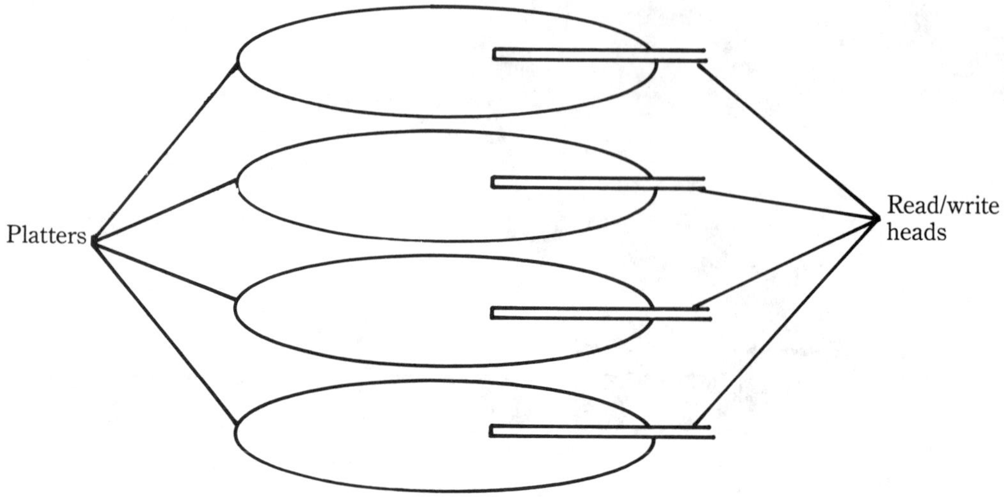


**7-1** Layout of a hard disk.

## Head

Like phonograph needles on a record, read/write devices called heads rest just above the surface of the disk platters. (If they touch the surface a *crash* occurs and damages the disk permanently.) The number of heads is usually equal to the number of platters of the disk. However, in some schemes, there are upper and lower heads, or twice the number of platters. (Examples of disk hardware configurations can be found on the inside cover of this book.) The disk heads are numbered from 0 to $n-1$, where $n$ is the total number of heads in the disk. For example if a disk has six heads, they are numbered 0 through 5. The manufacturer's data sheet should provide this information for your disk.

## Tracks and cylinders

Using the record analogy, the disk has a number of imaginary slotted *tracks*. That is, it has a number of concentric circles on which the data is organized sequentially on the disk. If we imagine a *cylinder* passing through each of the platters at a particular track we can see that the number of tracks and cylinders are the same (see Fig. 7-2). A cylinder consists of all the tracks at a specific track number. The tracks are numbered from 0 to $n-1$ where $n$ is the total number of tracks. For example, if your disk had 615 tracks, they are numbered track 0 through track 614. The manufacturer's data sheet should provide this information.

Hard disks usually have a special track or cylinder called the *landing zone* where the heads are placed before power off (called *parking*

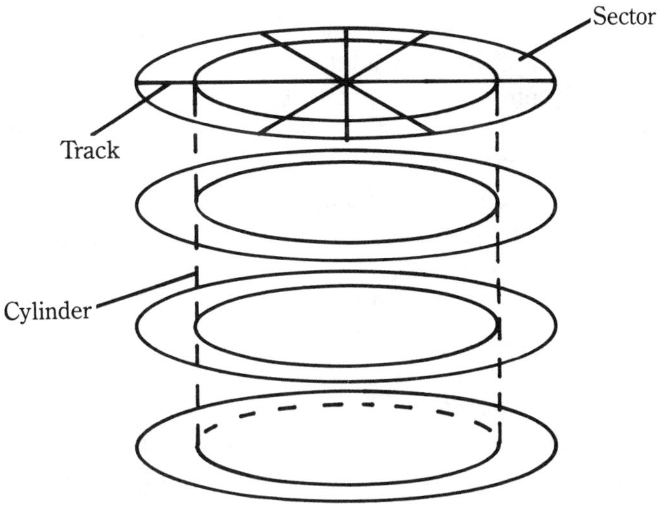


**7-2** Disk cylinder and tracks.

the disk). Most newer and large capacity disk drives park heads automatically—others do not. If your hard disk does not have an autopark feature, you can purchase a park utility or obtain one free from a bulletin board.

## Sectors

Each track or cylinder is divided like a pie into a number of sectors. Each sector usually contains 512 bytes (see Fig. 7-2).

## Clusters

DOS creates files in multiple sector units called *clusters*. Again the number of sectors per cluster varies depending on the BIOS version, DOS version, and disk media type.

## Interleave

As the disk rotates beneath the head, data is read and transferred to the CPU through the disk controller card. If the rotation speed of the disk is so fast that the data cannot be read and transferred quickly enough, a technique is needed to prevent data loss. Instead of reading from consecutive sectors, some systems read data from every second, third, fourth, or even fifth sector. The additional time gained by rotating past the extra sectors is used to catch up in the data transfer process. Disks that can be read in two rotations are said to have a two to one or 2:1 *interleave* factor. There are 3:1, 4:1, and 5:1 interleaves (and perhaps higher for very fast disks) as well as 1:1 interleaves for well-matched drives and controllers, such as for IDE technology.

Setting the correct interleave value is important in optimizing the performance of your disk. If the interleave is too low, the disk may have to rotate around completely to get to the next sector (since it can't catch up with the data transfer the first time around). If the interleave is too high, time is wasted rotating to the next usable sector since the data transfer process has already caught up. The manufacturer of your disk drive should tell you the optimum interleave factor, and there are also programs that will do this (see chapter 14). The interleave factor is set during the low-level format process.

## File Allocation Table (FAT)

The *File Allocation Table* or *FAT* is a list of allocated clusters on your drive. The FAT is used to allocate space for files one cluster at a time, to lock out unusable clusters (such as those residing in bad tracks), to identify unused or free areas on the drive, and to record a file's location. DOS keeps two identical copies of the FAT on each drive to provide a redundancy check and to protect against damage to the primary FAT.

The file *directory* is a dictionary containing information about files on your disk. For example, the directory contains a file's name, its date of origin, and the location of its first cluster in the FAT.

I am not concerned with the detailed structure of the FAT or directory in this book, but *The Norton Disk Companion* has an excellent detailed explanation of these if you are interested.

**NOTE:** When you delete a file, DOS only removes the first byte of the file's name and all its FAT entries. This is the reason that file recovery programs can be written. The actual data for the file has not been destroyed, and a "smart" program can recover the file if you have not created additional files in that space. If you accidentally erase a file, do not do anything else until you have recovered that file using one of the tools discussed in chapter 14.

Disk *fragmentation* is a problem associated with the continual deletion and creation of files. During the normal life of the disk, many files are created and deleted, and spaces or gaps are therefore created in the used disk area. A disk that has many such holes or spaces is said to be fragmented (see Fig. 7-3). Fragmented disks slow disk access time and—ultimately—computer performance, because when new files are stored in the blank spaces, they are necessarily broken up into sectors or clusters by DOS. When a file is scattered all over the disk, additional time is needed to retrieve it because often only a sector of data instead of a cluster can be read at a time, and additional overhead is required to

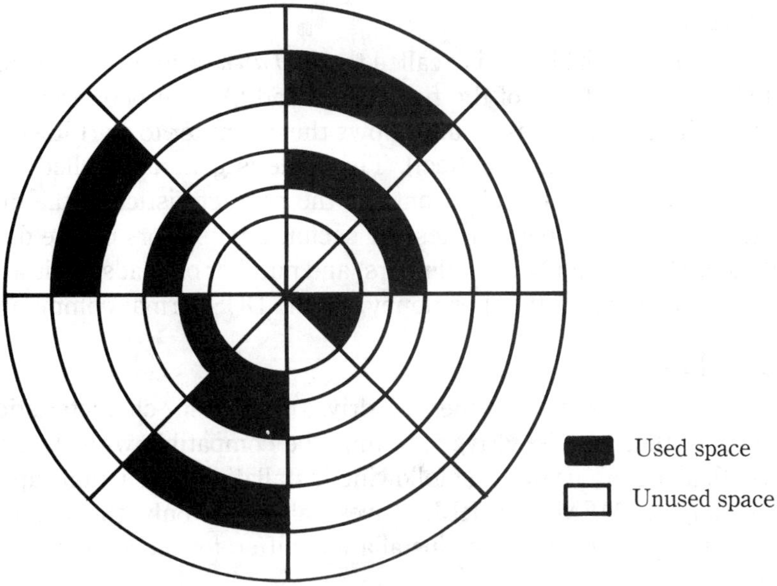


**7-3** A fragmented disk.

find the next piece of the file. Commercial tools are available to eliminate fragmentation by compressing or *compacting* the disk (see chapter 14).

**NOTE:** The command xcopy, available in some later versions of DOS, can copy files, directories and subdirectories. xcopy attempts to lay down the files contiguously. Thus by moving files around on your disks, you can eventually compact it. While xcopy represents a "free" compacting program, this process can be tedious and difficult.

## Partition

A disk *partition* is a logical section of the disk drive. Each partition can be assigned a letter and become a DOS-accessible drive. Disk partitioning is used when the storage capacity of the disk exceeds the size supported by the version of DOS you are running. Partitioning can also be used to divide the disk space for security or organization considerations. The *partition table* that contains this information generally occupies the first sector of the first track of the first platter (head 0) of the hard disk.

**NOTE:** In some environments, one or more partitions might be devoted to another operating system such as UNIX, and would therefore not be accessible to DOS.

### Boot area

A special area on the hard disk called the *boot area* occupies the second sector of the first track of the first disk (head 0). The boot area contains special code that essentially allows the computer to start itself up from scratch (its morning coffee!). This code is generally called *bootstrap code*. The boot area also contains the characteristics of the disk itself, including: number of bytes per sector, total sectors on the disk, sectors per track, number of cylinders, and number of heads. This area is created on any disk (hard or floppy) by the DOS format command.

### Types of drives

Chapter 6 discussed the types of drives and their characteristics. Remember that the disk drive type must be compatible with the controller that you are using. The following installation instructions apply specifically to MFM and RLL drives, although only the cabling, jumper setting, and physical installation differ for SCSI and ESDI drives.

## Installing/replacing hard disks

There are essentially six steps in installing a hard disk (see Fig. 7-4):

1. Setting jumpers
2. Cabling and physical installation
3. Running setup
4. Low-level formatting
5. Partitioning
6. DOS formatting

For SCSI, ESDI, or IDE drives, skip sections 1, 2, and 4 and follow the manufacturer's instructions instead.

### Setting jumpers

There are two jumper switches on your hard disk (found on the bottom or back of the drive) whose settings depend on which cables you have (see Fig. 7-5). For MFM disk drives there are two types of cables that connect the disk drive to its controller. The fatter cable is called the *control* cable and the thinner one is called the *data* cable. In addition, there are two types of control cables: straight and twisted (see Fig. 7-6). The twisted cable has an obvious kink in the middle.

When the 34-pin flat control cable is the twisted type, then set the jumpers for the drive to drive select 2. (This is still true if a second hard

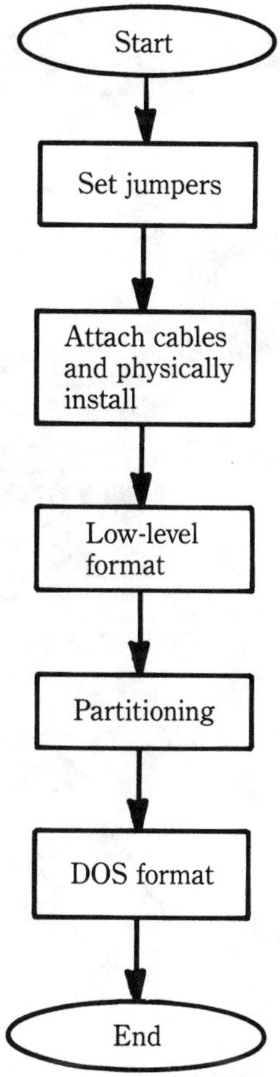


**7-4** General hard disk installation procedure.

disk drive is to be installed.) If the 34-pin flat control cable is not the twisted type, then set the jumper on the first drive (the one that will be drive C and is connected to the middle connector of the cable) to drive select 1 and the other to drive select 2 (this will be drive D, and it should be connected to the last connector on the cable).

In any case, only the last drive on the cable should have the jumper switch "TR" installed. If another drive is installed, its "TR" jumper should be removed. Figure 7-7 provides a pictorial description of the procedures. To review, the steps are:

1. Identify the control cable type.
2. Set the drive select jumpers.
3. Set the termination resistor.

**7-5** Location of jumpers on hard disk drive.

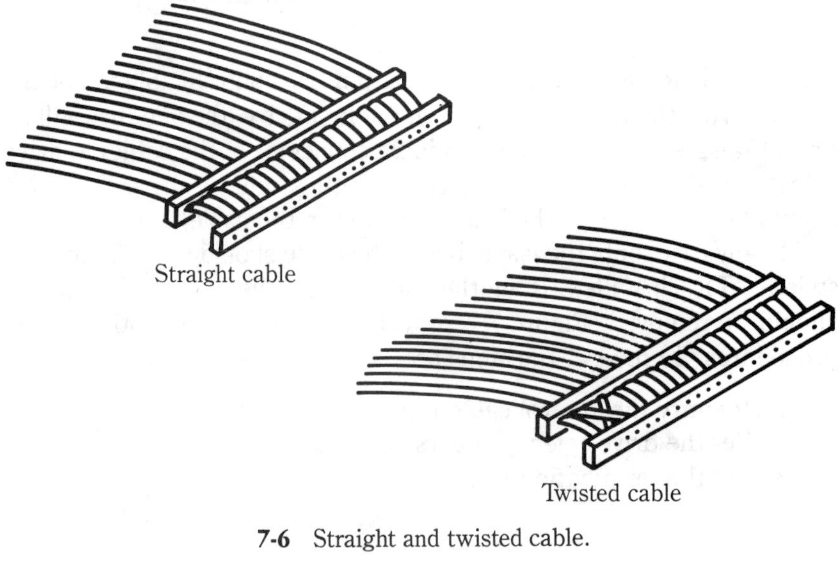


**7-6** Straight and twisted cable.

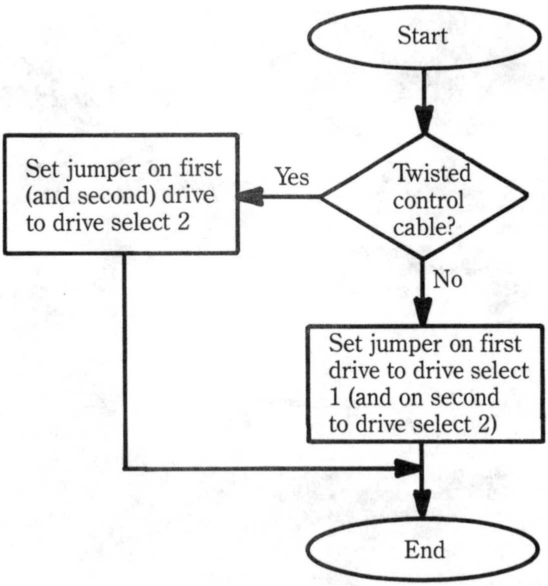


**7-7** Setting jumpers on the hard disk.

## Cabling and physical installation

After you have removed the cover to your computer, follow these three steps to physically install the disk:

1. Install rails and slide in disk.
2. Connect data and control cables.
3. Connect power cable.

**NOTE:** To remove an old hard disk, perform these steps in reverse order.

**Install rails and slide in disk drive** Two rails are attached to the side of the disk drive, and both guide and hold the disk in place in the chassis of the computer. Often they are marked "left" and "right" (see Fig. 7-8). Two screws secure each rail to the disk, and a third screw secures the rail to the front of the computer (see Fig. 7-9). You generally have to use trial and error to line up the two screw holes on the side

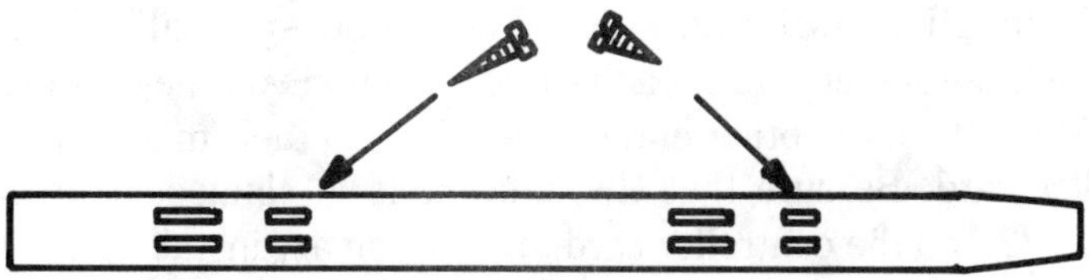

**7-8** Guide rail.

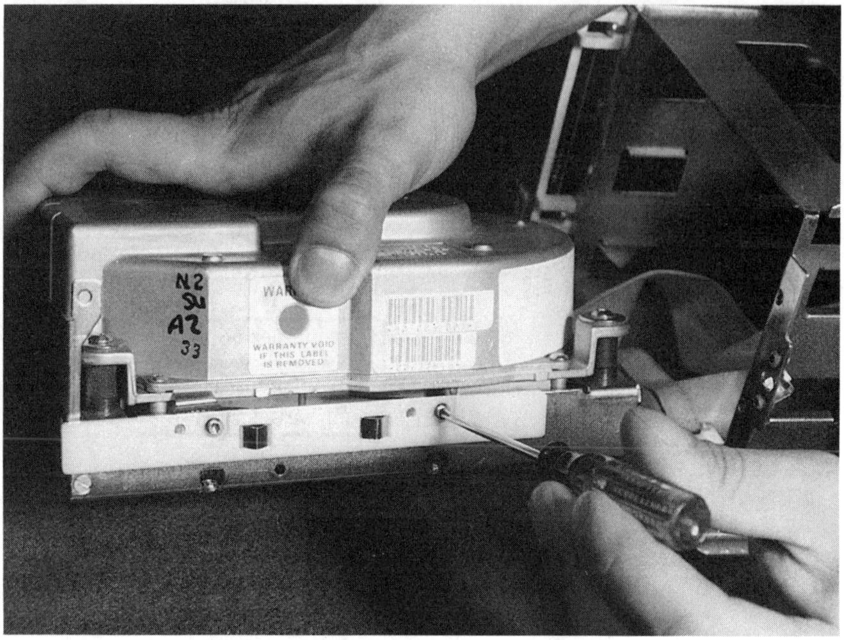

**7-9** Location of guide rails for the hard disk drive.

of the rails to the disk, in order to get a flush fit in the computer. Once you've attached the two rails to the disk and are satisfied with the fit, gently line up the disk drive so that the rail guides feed properly. Slide in the disk until it is flush with the computer's chassis and so that the screw holes line up (see Fig. 7-10). The front lip of the rail lines up with a screw hole in the face of the computer and the disk should be recessed far enough in the drive bay to allow the cover to be slid back on correctly. You can now insert the two final screws that connect the rails to the front of the computer.

**Connect data and control cables** Two cables must be connected from the disk controller card to the hard disk, a 34-pin flat control cable and a 20-pin flat data cable. Some control cables have a second daisy-chained connector in the middle to allow connection to a second drive, but in either case there are essentially two types of control cables: twisted and straight. The twisted cable has a twist in it that can be easily identified (see Fig. 7-11) while the straight cable does not.

Attach the slotted end of each cable to its mate on the disk drive (see Fig. 7-12). Attach the other end of the cables to their mates on the disk controller card. Be sure that the data cable is connected to the pins marked "J2" on the controller card, unless you are installing the second drive in the machine, in which case you connect the data cable to "J3."

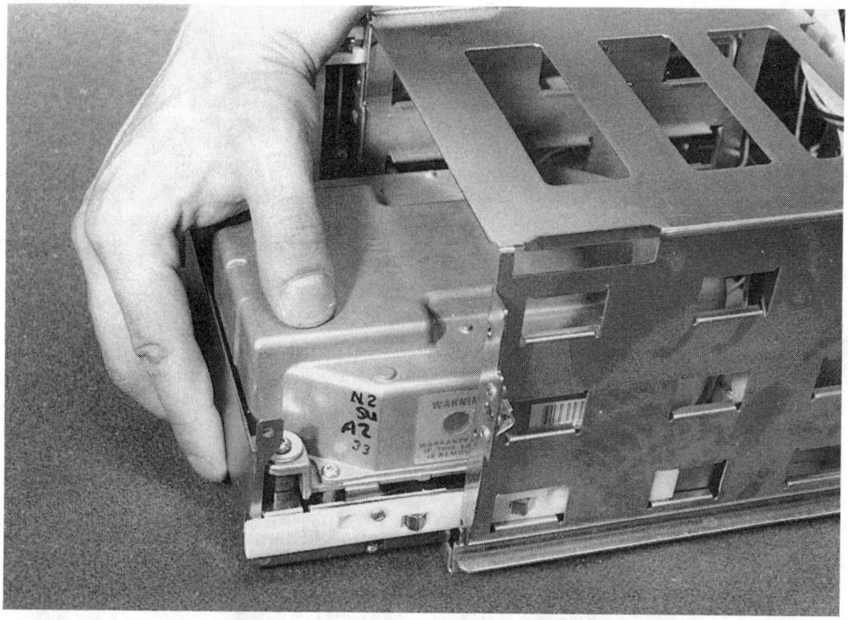

**7-10** Installing the hard disk drive.

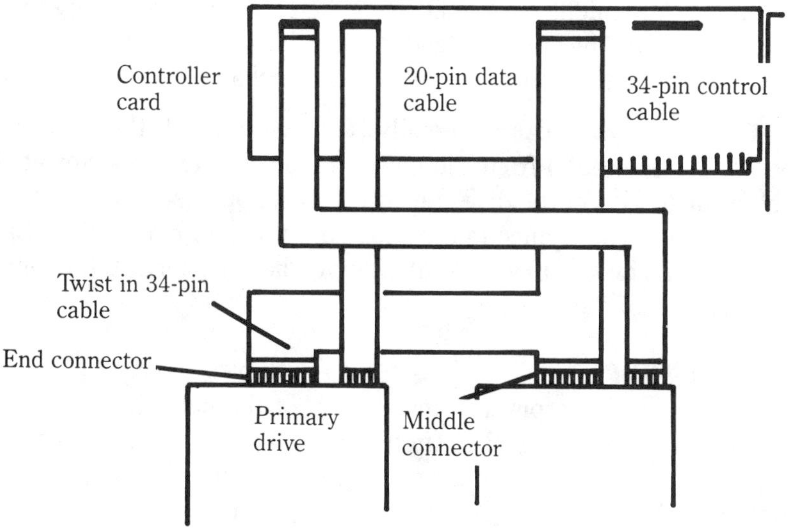


**7-11** Cable connectors on the hard disk drive.

Attach each cable so that the colored edge of the cable is nearest to the notched end of the connectors.

**WARNING!** *Be sure to use only the cables that were supplied with the hard disk drive.*

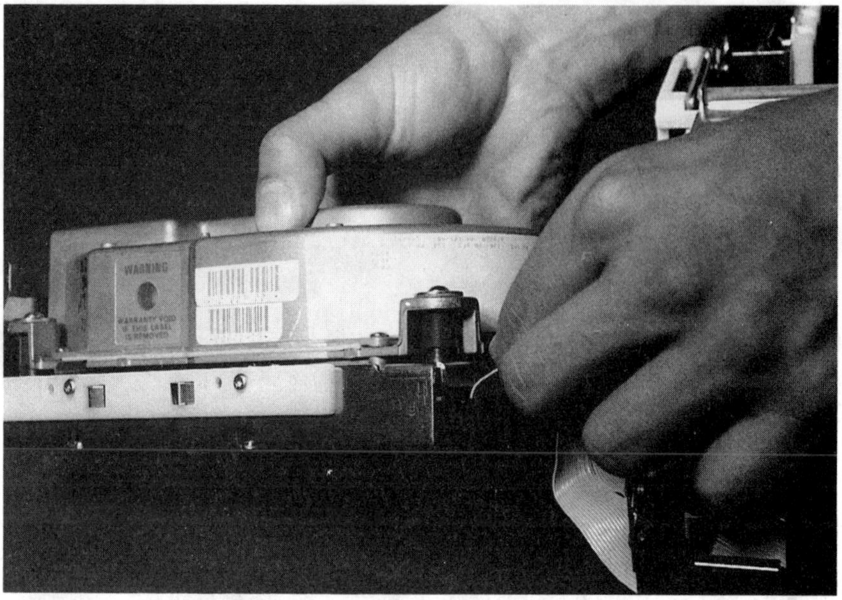

**7-12** Cabling the hard disk drive.

**NOTE:** You might want to connect the cables before sliding in the disk. In this case, be sure you feed in the cables so that when you slide in the disk the cables sit properly within the chassis.

**Connect power cable** Finally, connect one of the cables (it doesn't matter which) from the power supply to the connector at the back or underside of the disk. Be sure it is snapped securely in place.

After this final connection, you can put the computer's cover back on, or you can choose to wait until after you have performed the logical configuration of the disk.

## Running setup

After completing the physical installation of the hard disk, you must tell the computer's internal configuration table that the disk has been installed. To do this, you run the setup program and indicate how many drives have been installed and what type they are. You enter the drive type as an integer number, which differs from computer to computer (it is contained in a drive table stored in ROM). Selecting the correct drive number is important because it tells the computer the number of tracks and heads—and thus storage capacity—of the disk. Most setup programs provide some kind of online help to determine the drive number; if not, you must consult the computer's installation manual.

On older XTs and PCs, the setup procedure is replaced by setting jumper or DIP switches on the motherboard. In addition, you must load a device driver during bootup. The device driver can be added to the config.sys file. See chapter 13 and your computer's installation manual for more information on this.

**NOTE:** Unless you replaced an existing hard disk with exactly the same model, you should run the setup program.

## Low-level formatting

When the hard disk is delivered from the factory, the data area is not normally ready to be used in the computer. To prepare the data surface, the disk must be *low-level formatted*. (IDE, SCSI, and ESDI drives are an exception. Since they contain an integral controller, they are low-level formatted at the factory.)

**WARNING!** *Low-level formatting the disk will destroy any data on it!!!*

There are two methods for low-level formatting a disk. In older PCs and XTs, a special BIOS routine should be run manually from the DOS debug program (see Fig. 7-13). The other method requires special software that either accompanies the hard disk or the computer system itself. Both methods are discussed below.

**NOTE:** The effective storage capacity of the disk is reduced after low-level formatting by a factor that depends on the type of disk, the formatting program, and so forth. For example, a typical 80Mb disk might have 72Mb of usable storage area after formatting.

**NOTE:** The disk needs to be low-level formatted each time it is installed in a new computer and upon replacement of the BIOS.

**Manual method** The manual method of low-level format is used primarily on PCs and PC/XT-type computers. The procedure given here works only with Western Digital controllers, version 6.0 and earlier (other manufacturers might provide similar procedures). Fortunately, this is a very common controller type (the manual that came with the controller will confirm its type). If an automated low-level format is provided either with the computer or with the hard disk, I suggest you try that first.

To start the manual low-level format from the DOS prompt, type

```
debug
```

and press Enter. The debug prompt ( – ) appears. At the prompt type:

```
g=c800:5
```

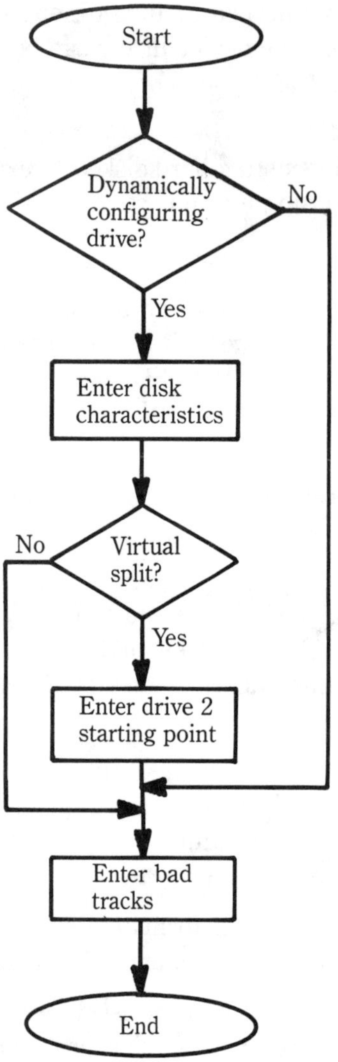


**7-13** Low-level formatting procedure.

The low-level formatting program displays a logo message. To change the drive to be formatted from C to D (or any other drive), type the new drive letter; otherwise simple press Enter. The program then displays a message indicating the current disk interleave. Press Enter to keep the interleave the same, or enter a number from 1 to 5 and press Enter to select that number as the new interleave value. Do not change the interleave factor unless you have reason to believe it needs changing; for example, if the disk manufacturer suggests it, or if a diagnostic program indicates that this is desirable.

The program then asks if you are "dynamically configuring the drive." At this point you have two choices: you can use preselected configuration (for 20Mb drives), or dynamically configure the drive (for drives greater than 20Mb).

Depending on your situation, proceed with the following instructions for either preselected configuration or dynamic configuration.

**Preselected configuration** At the prompt

```
Are you dynamically configuring the drive- answer
Y/N
```

select N. The next prompt will be something like:

```
Press "y" to begin formatting drive C with inter-
leave 3
```

Type y and press Enter. The program then asks you if you wish to format bad tracks (see subsequent section on this). There may be several other prompts warning you that all current data will be lost upon formatting; follow their instructions. The program displays the message "Formatting" while it formats the disk—a process that can take ten or more minutes depending on the size of the disk and the speed of the computer. The program displays a message when the format is complete.

After this step, proceed to the section called "Partitioning."

**Dynamic configuration** If you type Y in response to the question "Are you dynamically configuring your drive," a screen similar to the following appears:

```
Key in disk characteristics as follows: ccc h rrr
pp ee o

where:

ccc = total number of cylinders (1-4 digits)
h = number of heads (1-2 digits)
rrr = starting reduced write current cylinder
  (1-4 digits)
ppp = write precomp cylinder (1-4 digits)
ee = max correctable error burst length (1-4 dig-
  its) range (5-11 bits), default 11 bits
o = ccb option byte, step rate select, (1 hex digit),
range = 0 to 7, default = 5
refer to controller and drive specification for
  step rates
```

The program needs these disk characteristics (which should be available from the manufacturer) to proceed with the low-level format. Unless your disk is larger than 80Mb, the values for reduced write cylinder, write precomp cylinder, max correctable error burst length, and ccb options are left blank; otherwise use the characteristics specified by the disk manufacturer.

After you have entered these values you are prompted as follows:

```
Are you virtually configuring the drive - answer
Y/N
```

At this point the program is asking if you wish to do a *virtual split.* DOS version 2.0 allows drives of only 16Mb, and DOS versions later than 2.0 up to and including 3.3 allow only 32Mb. If you have a disk larger than 32Mb, you will have to do a virtual split. If you are not doing a virtual split, respond by typing `n` and skip to the section on bad tracks.

**Virtual split** If you respond by typing `y` at the previous prompt, you are prompted:

```
Key in cylinder number for virtual drive split as
vvvv...where: vvvv = number of cylinders for drive
C: (1-4 digits)
```

Then enter the value for the starting cylinder number and press Enter. If you have a 40Mb disk and wish to split it into two 20Mb drives, you should select the halfway point (for example, in a 615 track drive you would type `307`). The system then displays a prompt such as:

```
Press "y" to begin formatting drive C with inter-
leave 03
```

Type `y` and press Enter. Proceed to the next section.

**Format bad tracks** Most disks are manufactured in such a way that physical defects can creep in. These bad blocks or bad tracks need to be formatted by the operating system to prevent data from being written there. In DOS version 4.01 when a bad block is found, an entire *allocation unit* of fixed size (e.g., 2,048 bytes) is locked out. This permits formatting of a bad block without locking out an entire track. Although formatting bad tracks reduces the amount of usable disk space, it prevents data from being stored in a corrupted disk area.

During formatting the program asks you if you wish to format bad tracks. Respond yes, and Enter these in the form requested (usually as head:cylinder).

In each case a list of these known bad or unusable tracks must be given to the program. These are usually attached to the disk on a label or included on a computer printout that was generated at the factory, and might look as follows:

| HD | CYL |
|---|---|
| — | — |
| 2 | 123 |
| 3 | 256 |

This example indicates that head 2, cylinder 123 and head 3, cylinder 256 have bad blocks.

**NOTE:** It is not unusual for a hard disk to have two or three bad blocks. As a rule of thumb, it is acceptable to have up to two bad tracks for every 10Mb of disk space. For example, you would reject a 40Mb hard disk if it had more than eight bad tracks—this is a sign of potential trouble. (Finding twenty bad tracks on a 40Mb hard disk is not uncommon.) If the formatting program determines a disk is unusable, it will display a message such as:

```
TRACK 00 BAD -- DRIVE UNUSABLE
```

**NOTE:** During formatting the program sometimes displays a message indicating which cylinder and head is being formatted. Often when the program encounters one of the bad tracks, it hesitates and a grinding noise is heard. This noise is not unusual and should be ignored.

**Automatic method** As mentioned before, many hard disk and computer manufacturers provide low-level format utilities with their products. To use such a program, boot the computer with a DOS system floppy in the A drive. When the system has come up, put the utilities disk containing the special format program in the drive and start it by following the directions given by the manufacturer.

## Partitioning

The fdisk command allows you to partition your newly formatted disks into distinct regions. This is necessary if you wish to make more than one logical drive out of your disk, or if you have a disk larger than 32Mb and version 3.30 of DOS or older. In particular, fdisk allows you to:

1. Create a primary or extended DOS partition
2. Change an active partition
3. Delete an active partition
4. Display partition data

If your disk drive is 32Mb or less, or if your disk drive is larger and you have DOS 3.40 or later, then you only need step 1. If this is not the case, then you will need to perform step 1 twice, to create a primary and then an extended partition (you may have to do step 1 three times if you have an 80Mb disk). Figure 7-14 depicts this procedure.

**7-14** Partitioning a disk with fdisk.

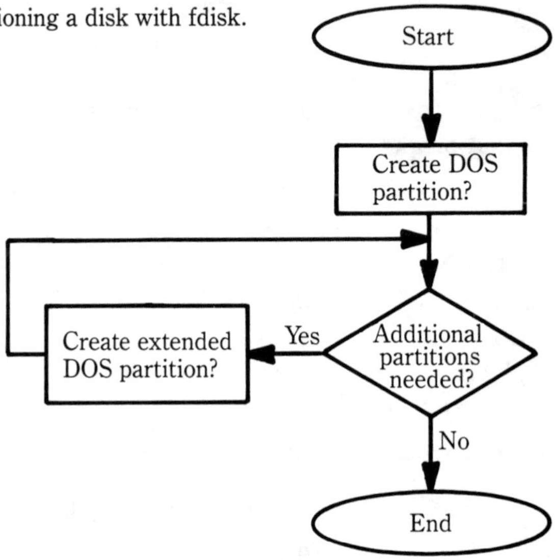


To run fdisk from the system prompt, type:

```
fdisk
```

You will then see a menu such as this one:

```
Choose one of the following:
1. Create DOS Partition
2. Change Active Partition
3. Delete DOS Partition
4. Display Partition Information
```

If you wish to exit fdisk without making any partition changes, press Escape at this menu.

**Create DOS partition** When you type `1` at the main menu, a new menu is displayed:

```
Choose one of the following:
1. Create Primary DOS Partition
```

2. `Create Extended DOS Partition`
3. `Create Logical DOS Drives in Extended DOS Partition`

Select 1 from the menu to create the primary partition. The program then asks if you wish to select the maximum partition size. Respond yes to this question unless for some reason you want a smaller partition size, in which case you are prompted for the partition size (or the ending head and cylinder of the partition). Creating a partition of less than the maximum size should not be undertaken except by an advanced user.

To return to the main fdisk menu, press Escape. The program automatically reboots the computer if changes have been made to the partition table.

Skip this paragraph unless your disk is larger than 32Mb and your DOS version is 3.30 or earlier. Run fdisk again and select 1 from the main menu. Select option 2, "Create Extended DOS Partition," from the next menu. The program then asks if you wish to create the maximum partition size; respond "yes." After you press the Escape key, fdisk automatically asks if you wish to assign a logical drive number to this partition. You should respond "yes" (this creates a drive D). Although there is a separate menu option to create logical drives, you do not need it. After completing this step, press Escape and the program automatically reboots the computer.

**NOTE:** If your drive is 80Mb or larger, you may have to rerun fdisk one or more times to create additional partitions with additional logical drives.

**NOTE:** The size of the partition should be less than or equal to the disk size.

Go on to the section on formatting.

**Change active partition** This selection (selection 2 from the main menu) is only used if you have partitioned your disk in such a way that one partition contains DOS and the other contains another operating system, like another version of DOS or the UNIX operating system (see chapter 13).

**Delete DOS partition** This selection (number 3 from the main menu) allows you to delete a nonactive partition. If you want to delete a partition that is currently active, then you must change the active partition (selection 2 from the main menu) first. If the active partition has not been made bootable, be sure to do so by following the procedure outlined in chapter 13. You should delete partitions only if you wish to repartition the disk completely.

**Display partition information** This selection (number 4 from the main menu) is used to display the status and size of the different partitions you have created. Run this after creating or deleting partitions to make sure your efforts were successful.

### DOS formatting

After installation and low-level formatting, the hard disk must be prepared to accept data in DOS format. The DOS format program is designed to do this.

WARNING! *DOS formatting the disk will destroy any data on it!*

With your DOS system disk in drive A, type at the A> prompt:

```
format C: /s
```

to begin the DOS format of your disk. The "/s" parameter tells DOS that you will be formatting the disk as a bootable disk, so that the two hidden system files and the command interpreter command.com will be copied onto the hard disk (these are explained in chapter 13).

Your hard disk is now bootable! Remove the floppy disk and reboot the computer to verify that this is so.

At this point you need to format any extended partitions created on the disk by using the DOS format command without the "/s" option. Do this for each additional partition created (e.g., disk drives D, E, etc.) by entering the format command for each drive to be formatted; for example:

```
A> format D:
```

After formatting drives, you should run the DOS chkdsk utility for each drive formatted to verify that the format was successful. See chapter 14 for this procedure.

## Crash recovery and prevention

If the read/write head of the disk comes into physical contact with the delicate surface of the disk platter, damage occurs. This event is called a *disk crash* and can be caused by a number of factors, such as mishandling of the disk or computer, running the computer during electrical storms, power surges, or turning the computer on and off frequently (e.g., every five seconds). If a hard disk crash occurs, the disk may be salvaged by a program like Norton Disk Doctor or by low-level reformatting, partitioning, and DOS formatting the disk. However, these solutions are risky at best, and possibly data on the disk will be lost.

When soft errors (no physical harm to the disk) occur, commercial disk repair programs can frequently solve the problem. Often, simply running the setup program again can solve the problem (a surge might have knocked out the computer's setup information).

# Repair

Once physical damage has occurred to the disk due to a crash, abuse, or some other problem, it is not readily repaired. Although there are companies that will attempt to rebuild the disk for you, or sell rebuilt disks, I do not recommend them.

Your best protection against physical and irreparable damage to the disk is to back up your disk regularly and to exercise your warranty rights to replace a damaged disk.

# Parking

By placing (or parking) the reader head of the disk drive onto unused tracks (called the *landing zone*), damage from head bounce, which often occurs when the computer is moved, can be avoided. Most of the newer disks automatically park when powered off. For disks that do not, inexpensive utilities can be purchased that park the disk head for you, and some versions of DOS provide a ship command to park the heads. In any case, the disk head(s) should always be parked before each power off and before moving the computer.

# Troubleshooting

The following hints might be helpful when diagnosing hard-drive problems.

1. Check the cables (including the power cable) to see that they are properly and securely connected. You might also try replacing the control and data cables. In the dry and dusty environment inside the computer, cables tend to crack.
2. Ensure that the jumpers are set correctly.
3. If an error like "Disk not found" is displayed, rerun the setup program.
4. Check to see that the version of BIOS you are running is compatible with the disk type you are using (see chapter 4 for a procedure for checking the BIOS version).

5. An error like "Missing command interpreter" means that a valid copy of command.com does not exist in the root directory of the hard disk. A similar message may appear if the version of command.com does not match the hidden system files or the version of DOS used to format the disk.
6. Try reseating the disk controller card (remove and reinstall it). A poorly seated controller card is the cause of many mysterious disk failures.
7. Persistent grinding noises are the sign of a bad disk or possibly a bad power supply. Both are serious problems, and the cause should be identified and corrected immediately.
8. Use the DOS xcopy command as a "free" compaction tool to enhance disk performance.

# Chapter 8

# Floppy disk drive

The floppy disk drive is one component that every microcomputer system now has, although some older systems used cassette drives only. This chapter examines the maintenance and repair of floppy disk drives.

There are two basic types of floppy drive units, the conventional $5^1/_4$-inch floppy disk and the newer, $3^1/_2$-inch "microcassette." Because they are essentially the same, I do not distinguish between them unless it is appropriate.

## Basic concepts

The floppy disk is a low-cost secondary storage device. It consists of a circular disk composed of a special material containing magnetic domains, and is covered by a protective jacket (see Fig. 8-1). The diameter of the circular disk inside the jacket is either $5^1/_4$ or $3^1/_2$ inches, which explains the familiar disk designations. The floppy disk drive is an electromechanical device designed to read and store information on the floppy disk. There are several concepts associated with the floppy disk drive that are similar to those for the hard disk, and others that are different.

### File Allocation Table (FAT)

The File Allocation Table on the floppy disk is created in much the same way as on the hard disk. See chapter 7 for a thorough discussion of the File Allocation Table.

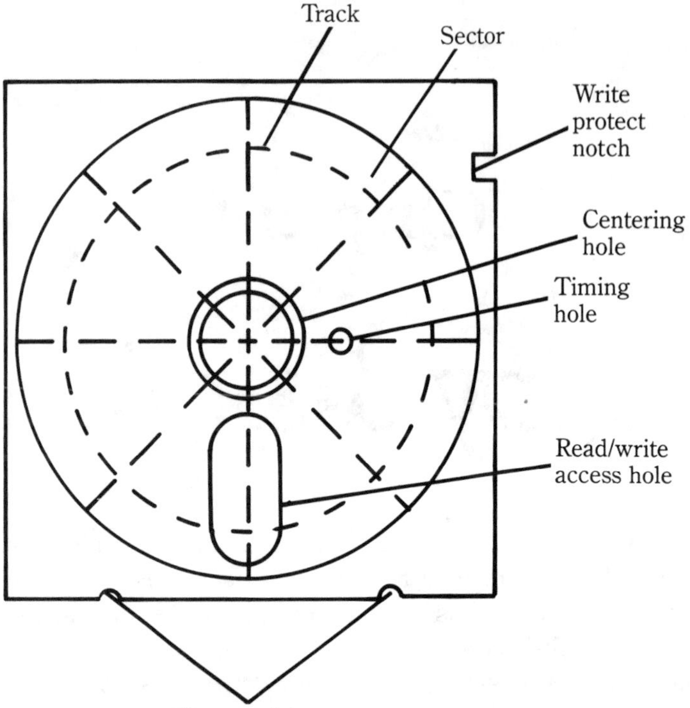

**8-1** Functional diagram of a floppy disk.

## Boot area

The boot area for the floppy disk serves the same function as that for the hard disk, with a few differences. On the floppy disk the boot area occupies the first sector of the first track of the first side. If the disk is bootable, then it contains the bootstrap code. It also contains characteristics of the disk itself, such as number of bytes per sector, total sectors on the disk, and sectors per track during DOS formatting.

## Tracks

Using the phonograph record analogy, the floppy disk has a number of imaginary slotted tracks. In other words, it has a number of concentric circles in which the data is organized sequentially on the disk. The tracks are numbered from 0 to $n-1$, where $n$ is the total number of tracks. For example, if you have 80 tracks, they are numbered track 0 through track 79.

## Sectors

Each track or cylinder is divided like a pie into a number of sectors. Each sector usually contains 512 bytes.

## Clusters

DOS creates files in multiple sector units called clusters. Again the number of sectors per cluster varies depending on the BIOS version, DOS version, and disk media type.

## Densities

Because of the technology used, floppy disk storage capacity is less than for hermetically sealed hard disks. The amount of information that can be successfully stored per unit area (density) is also lower.

Several common formats for floppy disks are based on tracks per inch and sectors per track. These numbers determine the storage capacity of the disk and are summarized in Table 8-1. These include the now extinct single-sided, single-density disks (SSSD) that usually held about 176K of data. Double-sided, double-density (DSDD) can hold 360K of data, while double-sided, high-density diskettes (DSHD) can hold 1.2Mb of information.

**Table 8-1. Floppy disk characteristics.**

| Disk size | Tracks per inch | Sectors per inch | Capacity | Acronym |
|---|---|---|---|---|
| 5¹/4 inch | 48 | 8/9 | 160K | SSSD |
| 5¹/4 inch | 48 | 8/9 | 360K | DSSD |
| 5¹/4 inch | 96 | 8/9 | 720K | DSSD |
| 5¹/4 inch | 96 | 8/9 | 1.2Mb | DSHD |
| 3¹/2 inch | 96 | 8/9 | 760K | DSDD |
| 3¹/2 inch | 96 | 8/9 | 1.44Mb | DSHD |

The disk drive types are upwardly compatible but not downwardly so. That is, a 1.2Mb disk drive can read a 360K floppy disk, but a 360K floppy drive cannot read a 1.2Mb disk. Of course, a 3¹/2-inch disk cannot be read on a 5¹/4-inch drive and vice versa.

# Installing/replacing floppy drives

The steps for installing and replacing either a 5¹/4 or 3¹/2-inch drive are the same. There are essentially three steps in replacing or adding a floppy drive to your computer system:

1. Setting jumpers
2. Cabling and physical installation
3. Running setup

## Setting jumpers

There is a single cable, which is either twisted or straight, connecting the floppy disk drive or drives to the controller card. (See chapter 7 for a discussion of twisted and straight cable types.) There is also a set of jumpers located on the back or bottom of the floppy disk drive (see Fig. 8-2). If you are installing a single floppy drive, and the cable is the twisted type, set the drive select jumper to drive select 1. If the cable is straight, set the jumper to drive select 2. If you are installing two floppy drives, and the cable is the twisted type, set both jumpers to drive select 2. If the cable is straight, set the jumper on the first drive to drive select 1, and the other to drive select 2.

**8-2** Typical location of jumpers on floppy disk drive.

In any case, the jumper switch marked as "TR" should only be installed for the last drive on the cable. If another floppy drive is installed, its "TR" jumper should be removed. Figure 7-6 provides a pictorial description of the procedure.

## Cabling and physical installation

After you have removed the cover to your computer, three steps are required to physically install the disk:

1. Install rails and slide in disk drive.
2. Connect ribbon cable.
3. Connect power cable.

**NOTE:** To remove an old floppy disk drive, perform these steps in reverse order.

**Install rails** To install the guide rails for the floppy disk drive use the same procedure as for the hard disk. Please refer to this section in chapter 7.

**Slide in disk drive** Gently line up the disk drive so that the rail guides feed properly. Slide in the disk until it is flush with the computer's chassis, and so that the screw holes line up (see Fig. 8-3). Secure the disk with the screws.

**8-3** Physical installation of the floppy disk drive.

**Connect cable** There is one control/data cable that must be connected from the disk controller to the floppy disk drive. Some cables have a second daisy-chained connector in the middle to allow connection to a second drive (drive B), but in either case there are essentially two types of cables; twisted and straight. The twisted cable has a twist in it that can be easily identified (see Fig. 7-6) while the straight cable does not.

Attach the slotted end of the cable to its mate on the disk drive (see Fig. 8-4). Attach the other end of the cable to its mate on the disk controller card. Attach the cable so that the colored edge of the cable is nearest to the notched end of the connector. In many cases, the cable is keyed so that a mistake cannot be made.

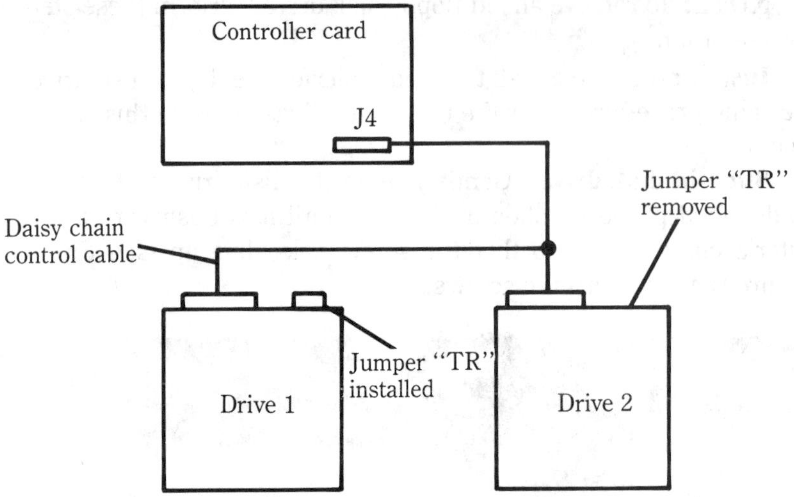


**8-4** Attaching the cable to the floppy disk drive.

**Connect power cable** Finally, connect one of the cables (it doesn't matter which) from the power supply to the connector at the back or underside of the disk. Be sure it is snapped securely in place.

**WARNING!** *Be sure to use only the cables that were supplied with the floppy disk drive.*

After this final connection, put the computer's cover back on.

## Running setup

After completing the physical installation of the floppy disk, you must tell the computer's internal configuration table that the disk has been installed. This is accomplished by running the setup program and indicating how many drives have been installed and what type they are. You enter the drive type as an integer number that is usually displayed by the setup program. It is important to select the correct drive number because it tells the computer the number of tracks—and thus the storage capacity—of the drive. Most setup programs provide some kind of online help to determine the drive number; if not, you must consult the computer setup manual.

**NOTE:** Unless you replaced an existing floppy disk with exactly the same model, you should run the setup program.

On older XTs and PCs, the setup procedure is replaced by setting jumper or DIP switches on the motherboard. See your computer's installation manual for more information on this.

# Crash recovery

Floppy disks don't "crash," since the read/write heads normally touch the diskette. However, data on a diskette can be destroyed or corrupted due to mishandling, age, temperature, and other factors. Diskette that cannot be read might be salvaged by using the DOS chkdsk command or a program like Norton Disk Doctor (see chapter 14). If these or other commercial disk retrieval programs cannot salvage the disk, then it is probably no longer usable, and should be discarded.

# Repair of disks and drives

Floppy disks by their very nature are designed to be cheap and disposable. Disks that have been damaged for one reason or another cannot be repaired and should be discarded, so periodic backup of all important floppy disks is important.

Similarly, the repair of floppy disk drives is not the norm, and replacing them is usually best strategy.

## Adjusting rotation speed

In some floppy disk drives, incorrect rotation speed can cause read/write errors. This problem can sometimes be repaired by adjusting the rotation speed of the floppy disk drive using the following procedure.

Take off the computer's cover, and remove the floppy disk drive from its bay by unscrewing it from the front. Do not detach any cables. Gently turn the drive upside down (the cables must remain attached). You should see a large flywheel that might have a pattern imprinted on it. A small screw should be visible near the flywheel that apparently serves no purpose of physical attachment. It is the rotation speed adjustment screw. Fluorescent lights (such as a desk lamp) do not shine continuously; rather, they pulse on and off at a rate that is some multiple of 60 Hz, like a fast strobe light. The pattern on the flywheel is designed to become clear at a rotation speed that is also a multiple of 60 Hz (360 RPM). Place a floppy disk in the disk drive and type the DOS dir a: command. The flywheel will rotate for a short time and the pattern on it will become blurred. During the time of disk rotation you must turn the adjustment screw one way or the other until the pattern becomes clear. The rotation speed should now be correct and the disk should be readable. Replace the disk drive and computer's cover.

If you cannot find a pattern on the flywheel or an adjustment screw, then you cannot use the above procedure.

# Cleaning

The floppy disk drive can be cleaned with special abrasive disks and isopropyl alcohol that can be purchased at any computer supply house. The abrasive and alcohol gently remove dust and dirt from the drive head. This type of maintenance can be done once a month or whenever a problem with dust is suspected.

# Shipping

In order to prevent the drive head from bouncing and possibly being damaged or misaligned during shipping, an old diskette or the cardboard dummy supplied by the manufacturer should be kept in the floppy disk drive slot.

# Troubleshooting

The following tips might be helpful when diagnosing floppy disk drive problems.

1. The problem might be due to a dusty or bad floppy diskette. To remove dust from the diskette, wave it in the air a few times. This method might sound curious, but it sometimes works!
2. Check the control/data and power cables to see that they are properly and securely connected. Try replacing the control/data cable.
3. Try reseating the controller card (remove and reinstall it). A poorly seated controller card is the cause of many mysterious failures.
4. Check to see that the jumper switches have been correctly installed.
5. Rerun the setup program. Electrical storms can disrupt the physical settings of the computer.
6. Problems with disks that can be read on one disk drive but not another (that is otherwise functioning normally) indicates that one of the disk drives is misaligned. To determine which one is misaligned, attempt to read the disk on a third drive. The two disk drives that are in agreement are probably aligned while the other is misaligned. Replace the misaligned disk drive. Misalignment, which simply means that the disk head is not properly aligned with the tracks, is usually caused by rough handling or frequent and prolonged use of the computer or disk drive.

# Chapter 9

# Video cards and monitors

This chapter considers the monitor or video display and its kin, the video card. Both are extremely important because the most interaction you have with the computer is through its display.

## Monitors

Monitors and video cards differ in the type of circuitry they use. The two most common are *Transistor-Transistor Logic* (TTL), and *Red Green Blue* (RGB). TTL is low-cost transistor configuration that uses five-volt logic levels and D-type connectors (see Fig. 9-1, Fig. 9-2, and Table 9-1). RGB is characterized by three cables representing the red, green, and blue lines respectively. RGB connectors are unusual for home microcomputers at this writing, so I discuss only TTL video cards.

Each different video card type is accompanied by a different system monitor or screen type. However, several *multimode* monitors, which are compatible with many different cards, and multimode cards, which are compatible with many different monitors, are available.

### Types of monitors

Monitors differ based on whether they are color or monochrome, as well as in screen resolution and connector type. Currently there are several basic monitor types.

The screen is composed of an array (matrix) of picture elements or *pixels*. The pixel density for the screen is called *resolution* and is given

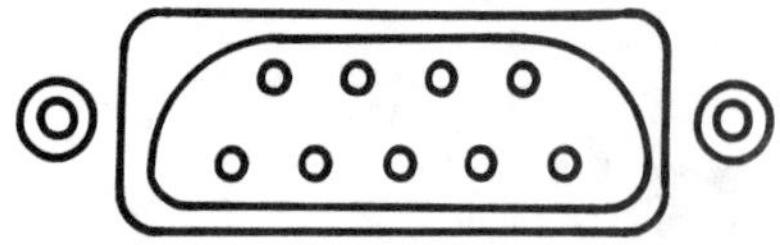

**9-1** 9-Pin D-type connector used for MONO, CGA and EGA monitors.

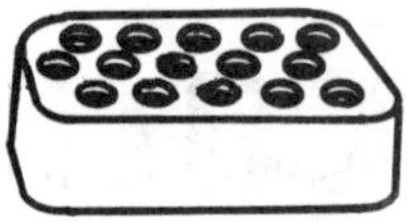

**9-2** 15-Pin D-type connector used for VGA monitor.

in the form x × y, where x is the number of pixels per row and y is the number of pixels per column. Table 9-2 shows typical resolutions for different types of monitors.

The monochrome or MONO monitor is a single-color screen that actually comes in many varieties including white, amber, green, cyan, and so on. MONO graphics monitors can support graphics and "colors" by using various shades of the base color and are typified by D-type connectors with 2 rows containing 9 pins.

The CGA, or Color Graphics Adapter, was essentially the first attempt at a color monitor for the PC, and usually has a D-type connector with two rows and nine pins. The resolution of such monitors is approximately 640 × 200 and they can support up to 16 colors.

The EGA, or Enhanced Graphics Adapter, uses a D-type connector with two rows and nine pins, has maximum resolutions of 640 × 480, and can support up to 64 colors.

The VGA, or Video Graphics, array card consists of a D-type connector with three rows and 15 pins. It can support up to 640 × 480 pixel densities, and 256 colors. This is the most popular card for newer systems.

**Table 9-1. Pin-out chart for 9-pin D-type connector.**

| Pin | Mono. | RGB | EGA |
|---|---|---|---|
| 1 | ground | ground | ground |
| 2 | ground | ground | secondary red |
| 3 | — | red | primary red |
| 4 | — | green | primary green |
| 5 | — | blue | primary blue |
| 6 | intensity | intensity | sec. green/intensity |
| 7 | mono video | — | sec. blue/mono video |
| 8 | horiz. sync. | horiz. sync. | horiz. sync. |
| 9 | vert. sync. | vert. sync. | vert. sync. |

**Table 9-2. Typical monitor types.**

| Mode | Resolution | Colors | Memory | Bus width |
|---|---|---|---|---|
| Monochrome graphics | 720 × 348 | — | 64K | 8-bit |
| CGA graphics | 640 × 200 | 16 | 16K | 8-bit |
| CGA (grey on black) | 320 × 200 | 16 | 16K | 8-bit |
| EGA graphics | 640 × 350 | 64 | 256K | 8-bit |
| VGA graphics | 640 × 480 | 256 | 256K | 16-bit |
| Super VGA graphics | 1024 × 768 | 256 | 512K | 16-bit |

Super VGA cards have the highest resolution commercially available for PCs. They use a D-type connector with three rows and 15 pins, and can support up to 1,280 × 1,024 pixel densities and 256 colors.

As mentioned before, there are commercial multimode monitors which are excellent, but they are quite expensive.

### Installing/replacing the monitor

With the power off, align the monitor connector with its mate on the video card (a 9-pin D-type connector for TTL) and press it in place. Tighten the screws to fasten the connector securely.

WARNING! *Do not force the connection!*

Some monitors are designed to plug directly into the system unit. If this is the case, do not plug the monitor power cord into any other receptacle. Otherwise, be sure to plug the monitor's power cord into a surge suppressor rather than directly into the wall socket.

## Installing a second monitor

Certain applications programs, such as CAD (Computer Aided Design) packages, require that a second monitor be installed. In this case two video cards are required. Each video card must be set to be "aware" of the other to avoid conflicts. Read the manufacturer's direction (for both cards) before attempting this kind of installation. Incorrect installation of a second video card results not only in video card problems but apparent CPU problems as well.

## Video cards

Each type of monitor, EGA, VGA, and so on, has a matching video card. (Although multimode cards will accommodate several types of displays, I discuss only specific video card types.) Video cards differ in bus size from 8-bit to 16-bit, and in the amount of RAM they have. In short, the larger the bus size and the more memory on board, the faster the display and, more importantly, the higher the resolution. Typical EGA cards are either 8- or 16-bit, while VGA cards are usually 16-bit. High-resolution VGA cards have up to 1,024K of RAM on board. Table 9-2 includes some common figures for different video cards.

## Installing the video card

Installing the video card is usually a four-step procedure:

1. Setting DIP switches on the video card
2. Physical installation
3. Setting DIP switches on the motherboard (or running setup)
4. Setting the application software so that it is aware of the card

**Setting DIP switches on the card** The first step, setting the DIP switches on the card, is dependent on the manufacturer's instructions and the type of monitor you are using. Be sure that the monitor type you have selected matches the DIP switch settings on the card. Furthermore, be sure that the settings do not conflict with those of another video card in the system. The manufacturer's instructions will help you here.

**Physical installation** Physically installing the card entails the usual procedure:

1. Discharge yourself by touching the computer chassis.
2. Identify a suitable slot and remove the slot cover, saving its screw.
3. Insert the video card carefully.
4. Secure the card with the screw.

**Setting DIP switches on the motherboard** In older XTs and PCs, DIP switches on the motherboard must be set, and in ATs setup might have to be run. Be sure to follow the manufacturer's instructions at this point.

**Setting the application software** Although many software packages can adjust automatically to any video card, others cannot. Be sure that any software programs you run are "aware" of the video configuration. The software's user manual can tell you how to do this.

# Troubleshooting

The following tips might be helpful in diagnosing and preventing screen and video card problems.

1. Check the contrast and brightness before assuming the screen is faulty.
2. Be sure that the software you are running is "aware" of the current video configuration.
3. Try reseating the video card (remove and reinstall it). A poorly seated video card is the cause of many mysterious failures.
4. Beware of bad power supplies affecting display performance. Wavy or "crawly" screens may be due to a bad power supply (see chapter 11).
5. Make sure that the DIP switches on the motherboard and card are set correctly. Be sure setup was run correctly.
6. Do not leave monitors on when not in use, because this practice can reduce the life of the monitor and cause permanent ghost images on the screen.
7. DOS commands, placed in the autoexec.bat file by you or by installation software, can affect the screen display (see Table 9-3). Check autoexec.bat for such commands and verify that they make sense in your computer's configuration.

**Table 9-3. Mode commands and their effects.**

| Command | Effect |
|---|---|
| mode mo80 | Sets display as monochrome 80 columns |
| mode co80 | Sets display as color 80 columns |
| mode co40 | Sets display as color 40 columns |

8. Installing two displays on the same computer can cause problems that don't look like video problems. However, some programs—especially CAD packages—requires two monitors. Be sure to follow the video card manufacturer's instructions carefully.
9. Try moving the video card to a different slot.

# Chapter 10

# Serial and parallel ports

The input/output channel for a computer is called a port, and there are two types: serial and parallel.

A serial port, as its name implies, transfers its data serially, or in single bits, or "signal events" (see Fig. 10-1). Serial devices on the microcomputer are based on the RS-232C serial standard. Typical serial devices include modems, FAX boards, mice, plotters and some printers.

The parallel standard for the PC specifies how an entire byte (eight bits) might be transferred in a single "signal event." There are other parallel standards, such as the HPIB, but their discussion is beyond the scope of this book. Since parallel devices can transfer eight bits (or a byte) at once, they are faster than serial devices. The printer is a typical parallel device.

While many computers come equipped with one or more parallel and serial ports, you may wish to add more. In this chapter I look at the installation and diagnosis of serial and parallel ports and their related devices.

## IRQ concepts

*Interrupts* are special hardware signals that are used within the computer to indicate that some special operation is to be performed. *Interrupt requests* (IRQs) are transmitted over a wire to the CPU, which responds to them via special software programs called interrupt han-

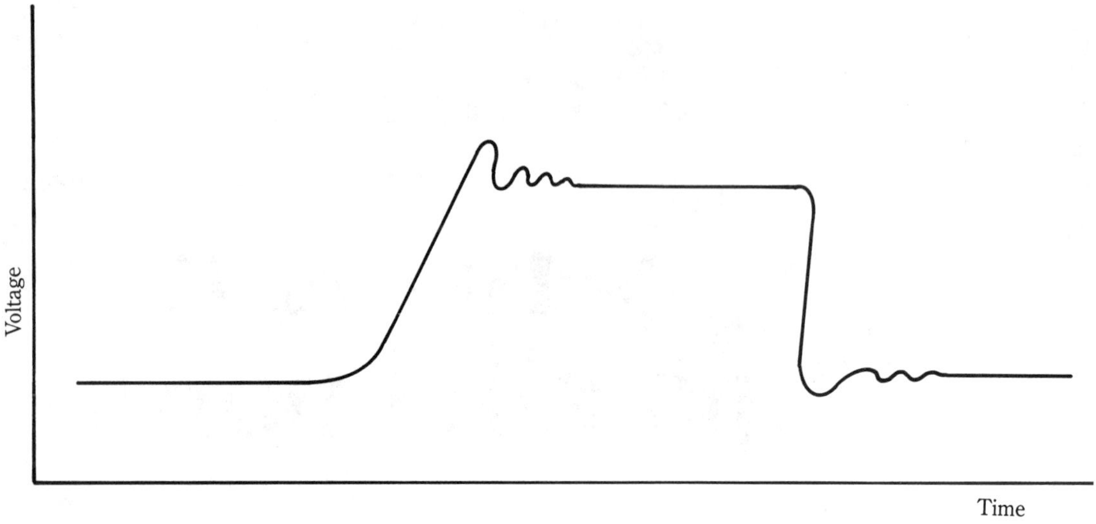


**10-1** Typical signal event.

dler routines. Each device, whether serial or parallel, uses interrupts to coordinate data transfer with the CPU. Since each device must have its own unique interrupt, the hardware allocates several interrupt request signals (abbreviated IRQ1 through IRQ9) as follows.

IRQ2 is typically used for the clock interrupt, IRQ4 and IRQ3 are reserved for the primary and secondary serial ports and IRQ7 and IRQ5 are allocated to the primary and secondary parallel ports, respectively (see Table 10-1). However, these designations can differ from machine to machine, so check the manufacturer's specifications. The other IRQs are used by the disks and other devices.

**Table 10-1. Interrupt request signals and their typical functions.**

| Interrupt | Function |
|---|---|
| IRQ2 | clock |
| IRQ3 | secondary serial port |
| IRQ4 | primary serial port |
| IRQ5 | secondary parallel port |
| IRQ6 | floppy drive controller |
| IRQ7 | primary parallel port |

# Serial ports

Many computers today have serial and parallel ports either built directly into the motherboard or preinstalled as part of a multifunction card (see Fig. 10-2). In fact, it is unusual today to find a stand-alone serial or parallel card except for *multiport* cards (cards that have many of one type of port). Often a serial port, parallel port, system clock, and memory are bundled together cheaply on a single board. The user simply disables any unwanted feature (such as the clock, which is standard on an AT) with a jumper connection or DIP switch. Nevertheless, stand-alone serial and serial/parallel cards can be purchased. Be careful, however, because these are manufactured specifically for ATs, PCs or XTs. Do not install an incompatible board into your computer.

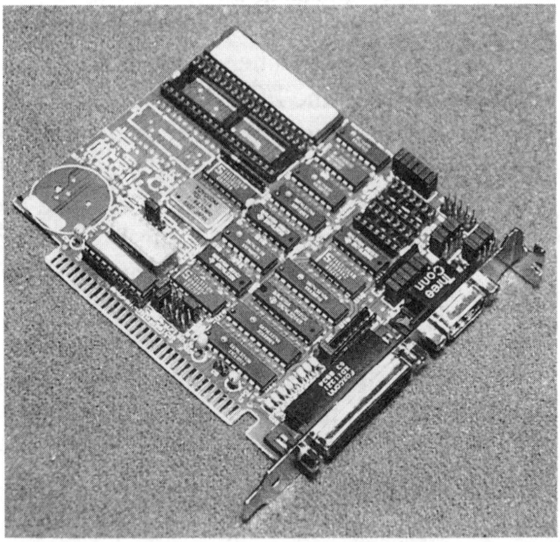

**10-2** Serial/parallel port combination card.

### Installation

When installing a serial card you must select which of the two serial interrupts it will be using. Ordinarily, IRQ4 is selected for the first or *primary* serial port, and IRQ3 is selected for the second or *secondary* port. If IRQ4 is selected, then the device attached to that port is referred to by DOS as COM1. A device attached to a port using IRQ3 is referred to as COM2. These selections should also be set in any software using the serial ports. Table 10-2 provides a list of DOS's generic device labels.

## Parallel ports

Parallel ports can often be found on video cards, especially monochrome ones, but again, parallel port cards can be purchased alone or as a part of a multifunction card.

| DOS label | Device |
|---|---|
| COM1 | serial port 1 |
| COM2 | serial port 2 |
| LPT1 | parallel port 1 |
| LPT2 | parallel port 2 |
| LPT3 | parallel port 3 |
| PRN | parallel port 1 |
| CON | keyboard |

**Table 10-2. Some of DOS's generic device labels.**

Most serial/parallel port combination cards support two serial ports and one parallel port. However, only one serial and one parallel connector are visible. The second serial port must be added by installing three chips on the I/O card and connecting a small cable to a set of pins on the card. These usually can be purchased separately as an "I/O expansion kit." After installing the chips and cable as directed in the instructions, the only other steps required are to feed the small cable through that extra opening on the I/O card that you always wondered about, and to enable the port by setting the jumper on the card.

### Installation

When installing a parallel card or multifunction card with a parallel port, you need only decide which of the two parallel interrupts it will use. Ordinarily, IRQ7 is selected for the primary parallel port and IRQ5 is selected for the second parallel port. If IRQ7 is selected, then the device attached to that port is referred to by DOS as LPT1 or PRN. A device attached to a port using IRQ5 is referred to as LPT2. These selections should also be set in any software using the parallel ports.

## Modems

A *modem* is a serial device that is used for transmitting information between computers and other devices over a phone line. "Modem" is actually an acronym for modulator-demodulator. This is a reference to the fact that the device converts the digital information of the computer into analog form for transmission over the telephone (and vice versa when receiving). Modems can be connected either externally through a serial port, or installed directly as a plug-in board. Some computers come with built-in modems, but in all cases the modem is considered a serial device. Modems typically come in several varieties that differ principally in the rate at which data can be transmitted or received.

Slower modems transmit data at 1,200 bits per second or *baud*. This means the device can discern 1,200 signal events per second (see Fig. 10-1). Normally we consider a signal event to be a bit, but in the transmission of ASCII characters over a modem we normally need for each character a start bit, eight data bits, and a stop bit, for a total of ten bits. For a 1,200-baud modem this yields a transmission rate of 120 characters per second. However, if some error-protection scheme like parity checking is required, or if two rather than one stop bits are needed, the number of characters transmitted per second is lowered.

Faster modems transmit and receive at 2,400, 4,800 or 9,600 baud (and faster) with correspondingly higher purchase prices. In addition, faster modems are typically equipped with automatic error correction and data compression (MNP 5 is a method you might see mentioned), or include software to provide this capability. Whether you choose a faster or slower modem, remember you can only transmit/receive as fast as the modem you are transmitting to/receiving from. In all cases the modem requires some sort of communications software that may be included with the modem or must be bought separately.

### Installation

Installing an external modem is simple: attach the modem to an open serial port on your computer with a standard RS-232 serial cable. Install the communications software according to the manufacturer's instructions and you are ready to run.

Installing a modem directly into the motherboard is a bit tricky, because you must select several items: the COM port and IRQ that the modem will be using, whether parity checking will be enabled or not, and whether one or two stop bits will be needed. You set these parameters on the modem card through DIP switches or jumpers. You must also configure the communications software to conform to these selections. The installation instructions for the modem and communications software, respectively, will help you make these choices.

Typically, the modem is configured as COM2 in order to leave COM1 as the open serial port. To do this, select IRQ3 for the modem if IRQ4 is set for the open serial port, or vice versa.

If your computer comes with a built-in modem, you don't have to worry about these issues.

## Mouse and trackball

A *mouse* is a device consisting of a small roller ball in a hand-held casing, and is used to move the cursor (see Fig. 10-3). The mouse moves

**10-3** Mouse and trackball.

the cursor when you move the mouse. There are two other types of mouse functions:

- Click: press and release a button without moving the mouse. Clicking is used, for example, to select an item from a menu.
- Press and drag: press a button down and hold it while moving the mouse. At the desired location the button is released. This is used, for example, to highlight an extended area of text.

For a two-button mouse, the left button is the select button, and the right button a user-defined function, menu, or help key. Three-button mice exist but are more complicated and their configuration and use depends on the software you are running.

A *trackball* is like an inverted mouse in that the casing is stationary while only the large ball moves. Trackballs are old technology for microcomputers now, but they are found on some laptops. Currently the *turbomouse*, which consists of a trackball and two buttons on a stationary pedestal, is becoming popular.

### Installation

Remove the foam plastic packing which secures the roller ball in place during shipping. If the mouse is a serial type, it is attached directly to a properly configured serial port.

If the mouse is a bus type, install it following the same procedure used to install a modem. In either case, some type of driver software, usually purchased with the mouse, must also be installed.

If you install both a mouse and a modem in your system, but sure they use different IRQs.

## Troubleshooting

Troubleshooting serial and parallel ports is an art from. You must have the correct cable configuration, drivers, and peripheral configurations. If all else fails, these hints might help.

1. You should try switching cables and/or peripherals to ensure that they are not faulty before suspecting the computer.

2. Try reseating the port card (remove and reinstall it). A poorly seated port card is the cause of many mysterious failures.
3. Check connectors and cables for bent pins. Bent pins can be gently straightened with needlenose pliers.
4. Communications problems most frequently occur because of incorrectly set IRQs or COM ports. Check these carefully.
5. One way of testing your modem is to use the modem software to dial your friend's home phone. If he or she picks up, you should barely be able to hear your friend's voice through the modem's speaker.
6. You can use the DOS debug program to make sure the serial and/or parallel ports are being recognized. From the DOS prompt, type

   ```
   debug
   ```

   which displays a hyphen (-) prompt. Then type

   ```
   d 40:00
   ```

   A series of numbers will be displayed on the screen. If the first line of numbers is all zeros, then the ports are not being set up in the system's equipment table. You need to check DIP switches on the I/O boards or motherboard, and/or run the setup program. Exit debug by typing `q` and then pressing Enter at the hyphen (-) prompt.
7. Try moving the port card to a different spot.

# Chapter 11

# Power supply

The power supply converts ordinary ac wall current into a form that can be used by the microcomputer. In this chapter I describe how to diagnose and replace a faulty power supply.

The power supply is easily identifiable as a large rectangular box, located somewhere in the corner of the microcomputer's housing (except in battery-powered laptops). Figure 11-1 shows the typical location of the power supply. Correcting a faulty power supply or replacing an inadequate one quickly is crucial because problems with this component can wreck all other parts of the system. One of the most common problems with upgraded systems is an inadequate power supply—one that cannot meet the power demands of all the components in the system. In this case, problems often disguise themselves as faulty disk drives or memory.

## Basic concepts

While I am not concerned with the internal workings of the power supply, it is important to mention the three most basic concepts in electronics: current, voltage, and power.

### Current, voltage, and power

In an electric circuit, charges called electrons are constantly flowing when the device is on (and the circuit is complete). When the electron energy level on one side of the circuit is different from the other, a

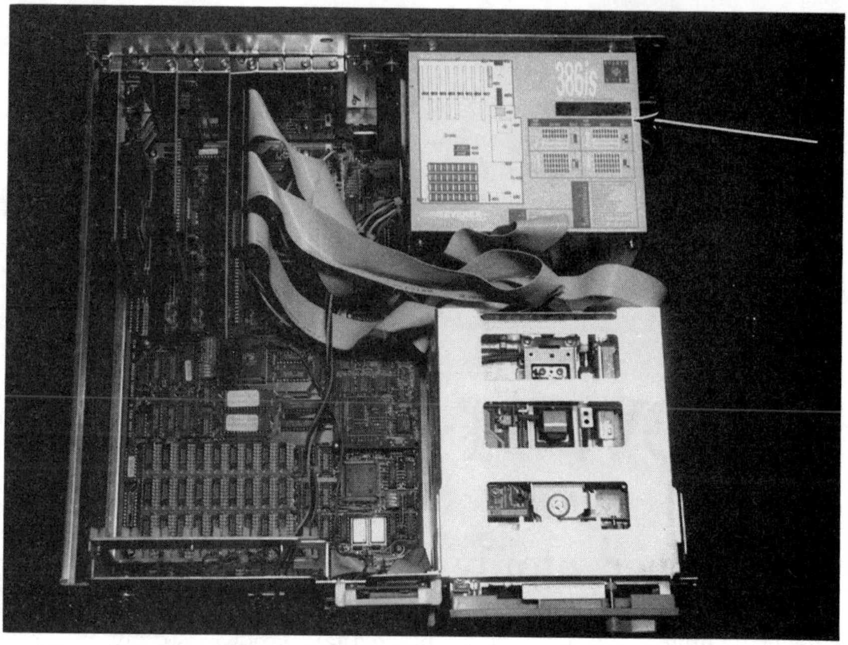

**11-1** Typical location of power supply.

potential difference or voltage exists between the two sides. If a path between these two parts of the circuit exists, electrons will move from the area of higher electron energy level to the area of lower energy level. When this occurs, a current is flowing between these two parts of the circuit. Thus current is the rate of flow of electrons, and voltage, in a sense, is the amount of electrons flowing.

The product of the current ($I$), which is measured in amperes or amps and the voltage ($V$), which is measured in volts, is called power. This relationship is given by

$$P = IV$$

Power is measured in watts.

Each time a device is added to the system, the power requirement is increased. If too many devices are in the system, the power supply might not be able to satisfy these requirements, and mysterious problems can occur.

Typical AT systems now have 150-watt and 200-watt power supplies as a minimum. Older PCs and XTs might have power supplies of only 60 watts. As a rule of thumb, make sure that the system has 50 watts for each hard disk, 20 watts for each floppy disk, and 20 watts for the system board. For each additional card, such as video, memory,

**Table 11-1. Suggested power allocations for various devices.**

| Device | Power allocation |
|---|---|
| Hard disk | 50 watts |
| Floppy disk | 10 watts |
| System board | 10 watts |
| Each card | 5 watts |
| Monitor | 10 watts |

and so on, allocate an additional 5 watts of power. If the monitor plugs directly into the system unit, allow 10 more watts. Table 11-1 summarizes these allocations.

**EXAMPLE:** A basic AT system with system board, video card, hard disk, two floppy drives, controller card, and I/O card should have 10 + 5 + 50 + 20 + 5 + 5 = 95 watts of power available. A typical 200-watt AT power supply has sufficient power for this setup.

**NOTE:** Most manufacturers of hard disks and other devices offer suggested minimum power requirements for their devices.

**NOTE:** A power supply can never provide too much power. It is better to have extra power than not enough.

# Installing/replacing the power supply

When installing a new or replacing an old power supply, be sure it is designed for the system in which you are installing it. That is, there are PC, XT, and AT power supplies that are not generally interchangeable. Be sure you purchase the correct one. Replacing an old power supply or installing a new one is very simple and requires the following steps.

1. Align and secure the power supply.
2. Connect it to the system board.
3. Connect it to devices.

**NOTE:** You can reverse these steps to remove an old power supply.

**WARNING:** *Be sure power is off and the machine is completely unplugged before installing or removing a power supply.*

## Aligning and securing the power supply

Align the new power supply housing with the screw holes that are provided for it in the chassis. Be sure it is well aligned or the cover will not fit securely. Secure the power supply with the screws.

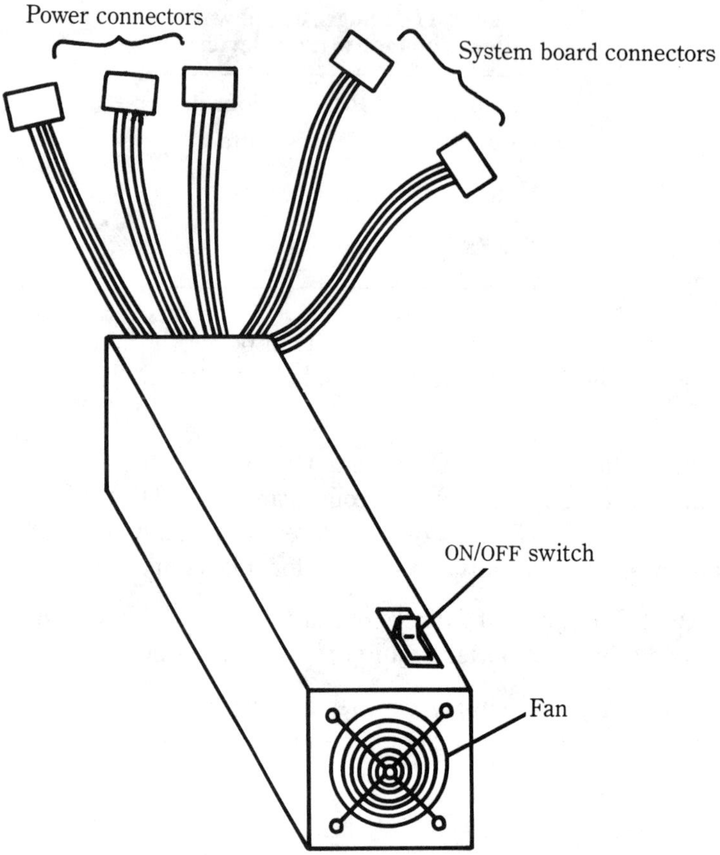


**11-2** Typical AT power supply.

## Connecting to the motherboard

Exiting the power supply are two cables with keyed connectors that must be connected to the motherboard (see Fig. 11-3). The sockets for these connectors on the motherboard should be within reach of the connectors. The cables are keyed so they will only fit in one way—the correct way. Do not force these connectors, as that can damage the system. If the connectors do not seem to fit, you might have the wrong connector, socket, or power supply.

## Connecting to devices

After connecting to the motherboard, connect a power cable from the power supply to each of the devices in the system (e.g., the disk drives). Again, these connectors are keyed so they will only seat properly in the correct manner (see Fig. 11-4).

**11-3** Power supply connections to the motherboard.

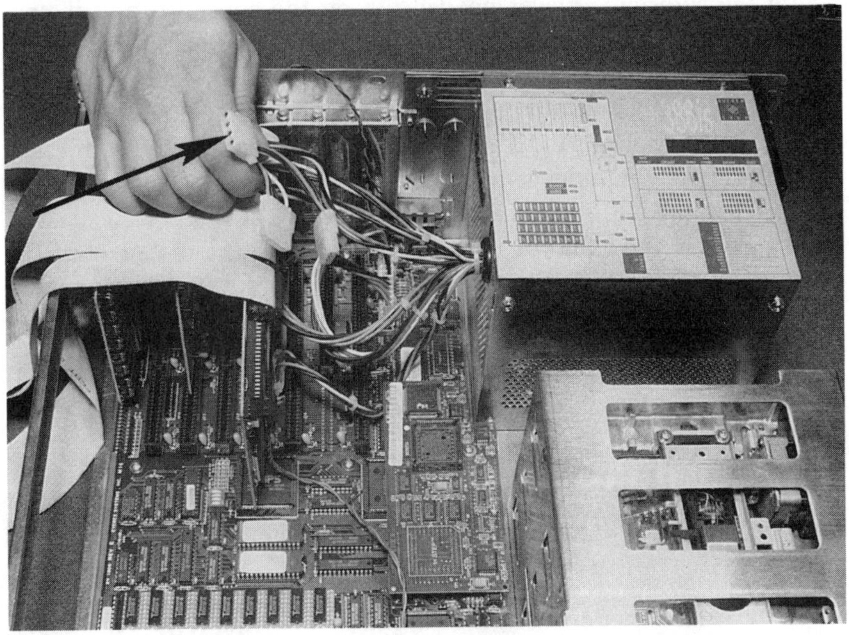

**11-4** Cables that connect power supply to disk drives.

**NOTE:** It does not matter which power cable connects to which device, because they are all the same.

# Repairing power supplies

Power supplies cannot be repaired by you, nor can they usually be repaired even by a computer service house.

**WARNING:** *Never try to open and repair a power supply if you think it is bad. Just throw it away.*

# Uninterruptible power supply

In chapter 2, I discussed the benefits of a surge protector. While a surge protector is important in preventing damage to your computer due to high voltage spikes or high-frequency noise, it cannot protect your system from problems due to brownout (temporary power drop) or blackout (total power loss). These problems are especially bad for disk drives and can result in crashes.

Fortunately a commercial device called an uninterruptible power supply or UPS is available to protect against these problems. The UPS is essentially a large battery that can provide power for short periods of time (e.g., 10 minutes) to enable an orderly shutdown of the system in the event of a blackout. It also can smooth over brownout periods, providing the additional power needed during the shortage, and it provides the same overvoltage protection as a surge protector.

Some larger systems come with a small UPS resident on the motherboard, but typically the UPS is an external device that simply plugs into the wall socket. The different components of the computer, such as the system unit, the monitor, the printer, and so forth are then plugged into the UPS. UPSs are rated in wattage or KVA (thousands of watts). Be sure the UPS you buy is rated to handle the system configuration you are planning. (See the section on current, voltage, and power at the beginning of this chapter.)

**NOTE:** Other external devices that do not user the computer's internal power supply, such as printers, need about 10 watts.

# Troubleshooting

The following hints might be helpful when diagnosing power supply problems:

1. The most common sign of a bad or inadequate power supply will be surging noises coming from your hard disk or repeated

disk failures on the floppy disk. Fading, flickering, shrinking/expanding or crawling monitor images are also a sign of trouble with the power supply.

2. Suspect the power supply only after checking everything else. Although there are ways to check the power supply directly with a meter, it is beyond the scope of this text. If you are experienced with a multimeter, then you might want to check this yourself.
3. The presence of power hogs such as electric coffee pots, copying machines, FAX machines, laser printers, toasters, or other computers on the same circuit as your computer can cause problems that appear to be related to the power supply. Be sure to eliminate these possibilities before opening up the computer.
4. If your system has a built-in fan, be sure it is working. A damaged fan can cause the computer to overheat, which can destroy the power supply (including the one you just installed) and other devices and chips in the computer.
5. Use only power supplies specifically designed for your type of computer, and that have an appropriate rating.

# Chapter 12

# Clocks and cables

This chapter considers two ancillary subjects: maintenance of the system clock, and recognition and use of cables.

The clock is used by many programs as well as by DOS for time- and date-stamping of files, so it is important that it functions correctly.

Using the wrong cables can result in improper operation at best, and damage to the system at worst. Frequently you might suspect major problems with your system when the only problem is incorrect cable selection.

## The clock

A battery-supported clock in the AT is used to initialize the DOS date and time. Early versions of DOS did not update the battery-supported clock, but relied on special utility programs. Later versions of DOS updated this clock automatically. The original PC and XT machines had no constant clock, but clocks could be added as a part of a multi-function card that also contained a serial and parallel port.

The clock counts pulses or ticks that occur 18.2 times per second. Thus your clock is accurate to $1/18.2$ of a second.

# Setting the clock

Usually setting the clock is as easy as using the DOS time and date commands. That is:

```
c> date

Current date is Fri 9-14-90
Enter new date (mm-dd-yy):

c> time

Current time is 11:40:01.93
Enter new time:
```

Separately installed clocks for XT and PC systems usually include a program with the product that must be run to set and read the date and time. This program or programs should be copied into your DOS directory and invoked each time in your autoexec.bat file. The manufacturer of the add-on card will tell you how to do this.

# Replacing the battery

The type of battery needed for your microcomputer varies greatly depending on the model. Before buying a new battery, you should remove the old one, take it to the store with you, and purchase either the same part, a compatible part from another manufacturer, or a battery that is smaller in size and shape but that has the same voltage rating.

Removal of the battery varies from easy to painful. The battery is always located inside the system unit, and can be loosely attached to the power supply with velcro, installed directly on the motherboard, or on a multifunction card. On some multifunction cards, the battery is actually soldered in place. You can either desolder the old one and solder in a new one, or buy a new card with a removable battery.

On other systems the battery resembles the square 9-volt type that can easily be snapped in or snapped out, or the battery is a large hearing-aid type. Some systems use standard AA batteries. In any case, the battery can easily be replaced.

After replacing the battery, run the time and date commands, or run the special software (included with your add-on card containing the clock) to reset the date and time.

# Cables

As I mentioned before, parallel cables are used mostly for connecting printers to the parallel port of your computer, while serial cables are used for modems, mice, plotters and other serial devices.

The maximum length of a parallel cable is severely limited—you can buy up to 10-foot cables in most stores, and special-order 50-foot low capacitance cables, but these are very expensive. Special long cable run devices are also sold that extend the effective length of parallel cables to beyond 100 feet, but even these are limited.

Serial cables are also limited in length to about 100 feet.

## Straight through

A cable with an RS-232C standard female-to-male connector wired so that the output and input pins (pins 2 and 3) of one are connected to the output and input pins (pins 2 and 3) of the other is called a *straight through cable* (FIG. 12-1). This type of cable allows two standard RS-232C devices to be connected to communications equipment such as a modem.

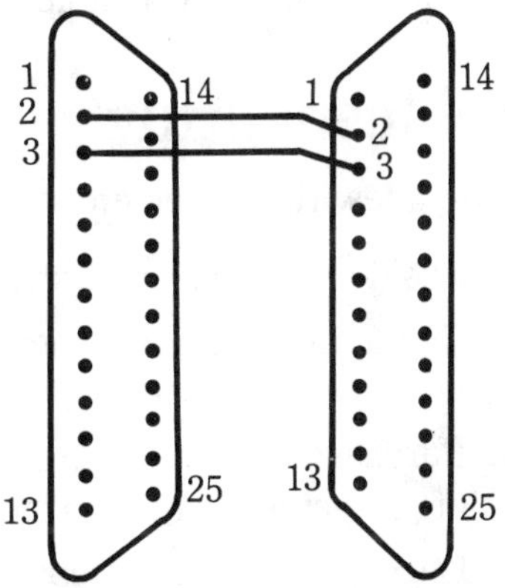


**12-1** Straight through cable partial wiring diagram.

## Null modem

A cable with two RS-232C female connectors wired so that the output pin of one (pin 2) is connected to the input pin of the other (pin 3) is

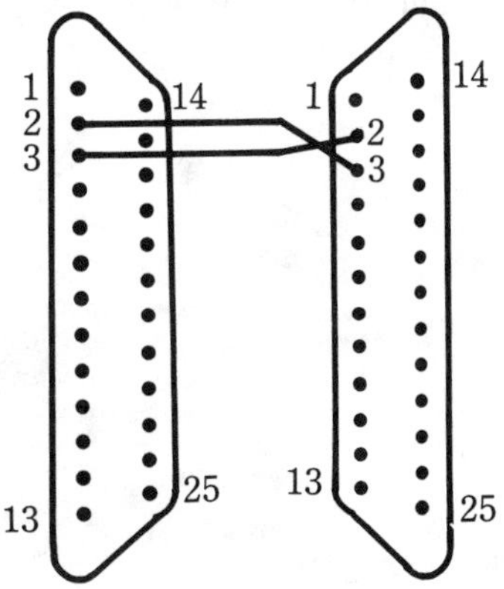


**12-2** Null modem cable partial wiring diagram.

called a *null modem cable* (FIG. 12-2). This type of cable allows two standard RS-232C devices to be connected directly without any other communications equipment such as a modem.

### Gender changers

Special devices are sold that can change the gender or orientation of a cable from female (holes) to male (pins). These are especially useful for connecting to devices with pin orientations that do not match those of your cable. Such devices are sold for 9- and 25-pin D-type connectors, Centronics cables, and even to change 9- to 25-pin, and D to Centronics, and vice versa. The use of too many converters to force a connection is discouraged, however. The more connectors and components in the system, the more unreliable it will be, and the more likely you are to make a mistake that could damage your system. Instead, you should buy a cable that is exactly suited to your needs.

## Troubleshooting

Here are a few tips to remember when working with cables.

1. Avoid spliced or taped cables.
2. Don't run cables near power hogs such as those listed in chapter 11.
3. Purchase cables that are "shielded." These provide some level of protection from interference by the power hogs.
4. Once you've figured out that a cable is working, screw it in, especially at home, where children or pets cannot inadvertently loosen connections.
5. Check cables for bent pins. Bent pins can be gently straightened with needlenose pliers.
6. Those familiar with a multimeter can test continuity on a cable to ensure all connections are being made.

# Chapter 13

# Operating system

This chapter examines some details of the DOS operating system as well as the nemesis of all computer users—the computer virus.

The hardware of the general-purpose computer can be reconfigured to solve different problems with groups of instructions called software. As I indicated in chapter 1, software is traditionally divided into two categories: system programs and application programs. The operating system is a specialized collection of systems programs that manage the physical resources of the computer.

In essence, the operating system provides a layer between you (the user) and the hardware (see Fig. 13-1).

The operating system used by most IBM microcomputers and compatibles is called DOS, which stands for Disk Operating System. Some microcomputers run an operating system called UNIX or XENIX, or an IBM proprietary operating system called OS/2. Older microcomputers ran an operating system called CP/M. DOS has evolved through several versions since 1982, with new features added along the way. Table 13-1 summarizes this evolution.

Some newer machines also support a special visually oriented operating system called Microsoft Windows. For the most part, the presence of Windows does not affect this discussion, because it runs "on top" of DOS. That is, it is really an application program. If you are running Windows, you need to bypass the Windows interface and interact directly with DOS. You can do this by selecting the "Command Prompt" option from the main menu.

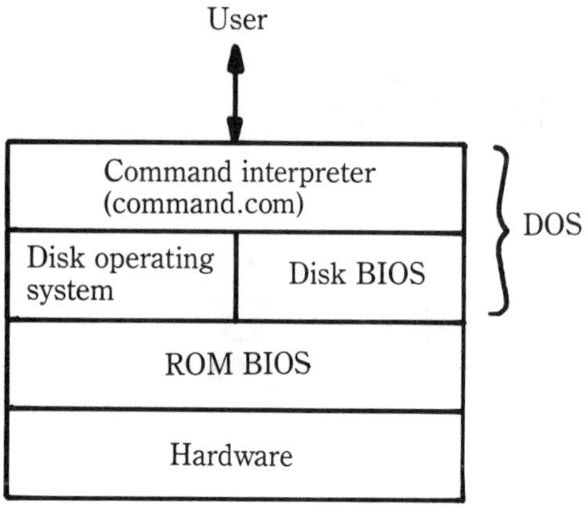


**13-1** The operating system as a buffer.

**Table 13-1. The evolution of DOS.**

| DOS version | Salient feature |
|---|---|
| 1.1 | Supports floppy disk drives to 360K. |
| 2.0 | Introduction of tree directories and hard disk support. |
| 3.x | Supports 3.5 inch disk drives and hard disks > 32Mb (version 3.4). |
| 4.x | Introduction of DOS shell and expanded memory support. |
| 5.0 | Improved memory management, full screen editor, enhanced DOS shell. |

# Installing DOS

Each time you add a new hard disk to the computer, if it is to be bootable, then you must install DOS on it. When the computer is booting up it will look for the operating system first on the A drive, and then on the C drive. If an operating system is not found, an error message like the one shown here is displayed:

```
system not found
```

If the disk was originally formatted with the DOS format /s command, then two special hidden files, called the system files, as well as the command processor (command.com), were installed on the disk. If not, these system files can be transferred from a bootable diskette to the hard disk by using the DOS sys command in the following manner:

```
A>sys c:
```

Once the system files have been transferred, the command processor file, command.com, needs to be transferred from the system diskette to the root directory of the hard disk. The command processor displays the system prompt and processes user commands. The command processor is transferred by typing:

```
C>copy a:command.com c:\
```

with the DOS system diskette in drive A.

Once the command processor has been installed, the hard disk is bootable. Test this by either cold- or warm-booting the system. A *cold boot* means turn the computer off and then on again; a *warm boot* means press the reset button or Ctrl-Alt-Del.

Now create a subdirectory called \DOS that will be in the default path. Copy over the rest of the files on the original system DOS diskette into the new subdirectory. Then copy the contents of the DOS utilities diskette to the same subdirectory. Finally, create autoexec.bat and config.sys files as directed in your DOS manual (these should be in the root directory). A brief description of these files is contained in subsequent sections.

**NOTE:** The sys command will not work if the disk was used after formatting. The hidden system files must be the first and second on the disk. Be careful of version compatibility.

# Upgrading DOS

When upgrading the operating system, the steps are exactly the same as for installing the operating system to a newly formatted disk. In fact, I highly recommend that if you are going to install a new operating system, you back up all data files onto diskettes, reformat the hard disk, and then install the DOS upgrade and restore the data files. Serious problems can occur if versions of command.com, the DOS system files, and other DOS utility programs are not the same.

# The config.sys file

DOS automatically consults the config.sys file upon booting (if it is in the root directory). Config.sys causes special programs called *device drivers* to be installed. These are software interfaces to special hardware. In addition, config.sys affects other operations upon booting.

For example, a typical config.sys file might contain the following lines:

```
device=ansi.sys
buffers = 20
files=20
```

These are four commands to be executed upon booting. The first installs ansi.sys, which is a screen driver using standard sequences defined by ANSI (the American National Standards Institute). The second statement in the file sets the number of sector buffers available in main memory. Increasing this number decreases the amount of main memory available to certain programs; however, some programs require this number to be set to a specific value. If you are having problems running these programs, check this value by looking at your config.sys file. The third statement in the sample config.sys file sets the number of open files that DOS can access at any one time. Again, certain programs require that this number be set to some minimum value.

Specialty drivers, such as those that extend the addressable disk size for DOS versions 3.3 and older from 32Mb to sizes greater than that, are installed using the config.sys file.

Problems can often be caused in other programs by the drivers loaded in config.sys. As a first step in debugging a mysterious software problem, you must bypass the config.sys drivers. This can be done by renaming config.sys (e.g., xconfig.sys) and rebooting. Then test the software problem; if it has gone away, the problem is in config.sys. One by one, add drivers to the config.sys file and reboot the system. In this way the offending driver can be identified.

# The autoexec.bat file

The autoexec.bat file is a batch file (note the .bat extension) that contains a series of DOS commands that are always executed upon booting (if the file resides in the root directory). Such files are used to configure your DOS environment automatically and consistently. For example, here is a sample autoexec.bat file:

```
prompt=$p$g
path c:\dos;c:\;
SET GMK4=D:\G4\
```

The first line is used to tell the system that the identity of the current directory should be displayed as part of the prompt, for example:

```
C:\book3>
```

shows that the user is currently in the subdirectory "book3."

The second line depicted in the sample autoexec.bat file sets up the path for the computer, that is the locations and order in which the system should look for files as a default. The directories listed in the path are searched from left to right until the file is found. Setting up the path in the correct order is important, and an incorrectly ordered path can cause problems when several files with the same name but different functions reside in different directories.

The last line in the sample autoexec.bat sets a global variable or parameter that can be accessed by any program, but typically has meaning for only one program. Commercial packages set up global variables upon installation to help them remember the hardware configuration of your system, or some option you have set. It is not a good idea to change any of these global parameters unless instructed to do so by a program manual.

Incidentally, the order of the commands in autoexec.bat does not matter unless one depends on another.

Often something in the autoexec.bat file, such as an incorrectly set path or a global variable whose value has been overwritten, can cause problems that seem like hardware problems. When troubleshooting hardware, it is good practice to disable the effects of the autoexec.bat file by renaming it (e.g., autoexec.old) and then rebooting.

Your DOS manual contains more information on building the autoexec.bat file, and most programs either automatically set up special commands in the file or tell you how to do it yourself.

**NOTE:** It's a good idea to put chkdsk with the "/f" option in the autoexec.bat file to automatically check for lost clusters upon booting. See chapter 14.

# The system files

Two special files (whose names vary from system to system, but are usually some variation of io.com and sys.com) are called *system files* and must reside on any bootable disk (hard or floppy) in the root directory. These files are *hidden*, that is, you cannot see them with an ordinary DOS dir (directory) command nor should you type them out. These files are transferred to a disk by using the DOS sys command.

# Viruses

It is unfortunate that certain persons take pleasure in the creation of programs whose sole intent is to destroy the work of others, that is, *viruses*. These programs, which are becoming increasingly more common, vary widely in their appearance, mode of transmittal, and destructiveness. Often the effects of viruses can resemble hardware trouble, thus causing endless aggravation with no resolution.

## Virus transmittal

Viruses are propagated through shareware, bulletin boards, and by the passing of disks that are not genuine. Some viruses have actually been known to have been planted on distribution disks, although this is uncommon. Others have been deviously hidden on "demo" diskettes and sent via the mail.

## Effects of viruses

The actual damage that can be caused by a computer virus ranges from none to complete low-level reformat of your hard disk. (There is no possible way to perform physical damage to the computer through a virus). There are literally hundreds of known viruses and variants of those viruses that can infect hard or floppy disks. Some typical effects of viruses are:

- Random screen flickering
- Random warm booting of computer
- File allocation errors
- Strange messages displayed randomly
- Deletion and renaming of files
- Destruction or alteration of the FAT
- Destruction or alteration of boot sectors
- "Sector not found" errors
- "Drive not found" errors
- Slower system performance
- Apparent CPU hangups
- Lost clusters

There are many more. Recognizing these effects may help you distinguish actual hardware problems from those caused by viruses. If you see these errors, and you have reason to believe you may have introduced a virus into your system, attempt to eliminate the virus before making any hardware changes.

## Antidotes

The first cure for a computer virus is not to get one. Following these suggestions will limit your exposure to computer viruses:

- Don't use shareware (unless it is certified virus free).
- Don't download software from bulletin boards (unless it is certified virus free).
- Don't accept software through the mail from unknown vendors.

- Don't accept software—from friends or otherwise—on nondistribution disks.
- Don't allow unlimited access to your computer.

A number of commercial antiviral programs are available that are known to be highly successful against certain known viruses. However, each program is not successful against all viruses. A sampling of these programs is:

- Dr. Solomon's Anti-virus Toolkit
- IBM Scan
- Pro-Scan (McAfee Associates)
- ViruScan (McAfee Associates)
- VirexPC (MicroCom)

Other programs available through shareware will disinfect one or more specific viruses. However, since they are available through shareware or other means of transmittal favored by viruses, use them at your own risk. In addition, an extensive virus information list is available through bulletin boards or by mail.

# Chapter 14

# Useful software tools

Several software tools are provided with DOS that can be used to aid in the diagnosis and repair of your computer's disk subsystem (the disk and its controller card). Additionally, commercial products are available to diagnose various system components and to perform logical repairs to disks. I briefly examine some DOS utilities and some commercial products with which I am familiar.

## DOS utilities

The diagnostic and repair programs included with DOS are limited, and vary in capability from version to version. Complete descriptions of these utilities can be found in your DOS manual.

### backup/restore

DOS comes equipped with two utility programs, backup and restore used for (what else?) backing up and restoring the hard disk. Instructions for their use can be found in your DOS manual. However, I do not recommend these programs for those running DOS versions 3.3 or lower. Instead, use one of the commercial backup and restore utilities such as Norton Backup or Fastback. These programs provide data compression to reduce the number of backup disks required, provide selective and incremental backups (in this case the system clock must be correct), allow backups from/to different directories, and are generally reliable. These features are not provided by the DOS utilities.

## chkdsk

I previously mentioned using the DOS chkdsk command to determine the amount of available or free memory in the computer system (see chapter 4). But chkdsk (the "check disk" diagnostic utility) can also provide useful information about the status of your disk, and with the "/f" option, can repair certain errors such as lost clusters. Lost clusters often occur when programs are aborted with files open or during power outages.

chkdsk takes an optional drive argument, or defaults to the current drive. It is illustrated as follows:

```
C> chkdsk/f

33435648 bytes total disk space
   55296 bytes in 3 hidden files
  124928 bytes in 52 directories
20762624 bytes in 1796 user files
   20480 bytes in bad sectors
12472320 bytes available on disk

  655360 bytes total memory
  594320 bytes free
```

If chkdsk finds lost clusters, it will ask if you want to convert them to files. If you respond "yes," several files named file0000, file0001, and so on will be created. You can then inspect these files to see if the information is indeed lost and useful.

**NOTE:** The "/f" option must be used in order to make repairs, otherwise chkdsk is just a diagnostic.

Since it only takes a few moments to run, chkdsk should be run every day with the "/f" option. (You might want to put it in your autoexec.bat file.)

### recover

Later versions of DOS provide the recover command, which can be used to selectively repair files that have been deemed bad by chkdsk. The recover command causes DOS to read the file sector by sector and skip the bad sectors. To recover a file named *file.bad*, you would follow this sequence:

```
C> recover file.bad

Press any key to begin recovery of the
file(s) on drive C:

1945 of 1945 bytes recovered
```

recover can take a file name (including wild cards) or a drive name as an argument.

### label

The DOS label command allows you to set a volume label for any hard drive or floppy diskette. The label command is invoked as follows:

```
C> label

Volume in drive C is none

Volume label (11 characters, ENTER for none)? PHIL
```

Volume labels help you quickly identify and keep track of many hard or floppy disks.

### ver

The DOS ver command will tell you the version number of the DOS you are using. The version number is extremely important in determining the compatibility of certain hardware and programs. The command is invoked as follows:

```
C> ver
 MS-DOS Version 3.30
```

If a mismatch occurs between the version of the DOS installed (the hidden system files) and the version of command.com, you should completely reformat your disk at the DOS level, and reinstall DOS and all application software. Be sure to back up all your data first, as formatting will destroy all the data on the disk.

### vol

The DOS vol or volume command gives you the name of the current disk volume. The default parameter is the current volume. An optional parameter can be set to specify a different volume. The use of the vol command is illustrated below.

```
C> vol c:
 Volume in drive C is PHIL
```

## Norton Utilities

The Norton Utilities have become legendary for their ability to perform file recovery and logical disk repair. These utilities also include programs that perform safe disk formats, do batch file enhancement, and provide system information. Other Norton products perform disk backup and recover in a fashion superior to the DOS backup and restore programs. To summarize, Norton Utilities include, among other features, the ability to perform

- disk diagnosis and repair
- disk compaction (reduction of fragmentation)
- interleave adjustment
- unformat and unerase for restoring accidentally deleted files and accidentally formatted disks (using a special "safe" format)
- batch file enhancement
- file search and information
- directory sort (sorts your directories in any order you choose)

# PC Tools Deluxe

This program combines certain personal management features such as calendars, database, and autodialer with practical diagnostic tools such as file recovery, logical disk repair, and backup. In addition, it includes its own window-like interface. To summarize, PC Tools Deluxe includes

- disk repair utility
- tape backup unit support
- DOS command line (previous commands can be "remembered")
- file unerase
- file backup and restore (superior to DOS's)
- FAX board support
- enhanced disk cache (for improved hard disk access)

# HELPME

HELPME is a diagnostic utility program that can be used with the IBM PC/XT/AT clones, compatibles, and the PS/2. HELPME can run over 300 diagnostic programs that include such functions as

- checking the integrity of files such as config.sys and autoexec.bat
- performing disk compression and diagnostics
- testing the hardware environment
- removing zero length, duplicate entry, and backup files

# SpinRite

SpinRite is an excellent program that will perform disk diagnostics, informing you of the disk's current and optimum characteristics. The program can compact your disk and a do a low-level reformat for the optimum interleave *without loss of data*. This feature appears to be unique for these types of programs. The program is relatively simple to use but can take several hours to run. Nevertheless, this program is definitely worth having.

# Other utilities

There is an ever growing list of PC tools, tutorials, help utilities, and other programs designed for the IBM PC family of computers. It would be impossible to list or review all of them here. You should consult popular personal computing magazines for reviews of the various products on the market, and decide which are best for you.

# Appendix
# Partial ASCII table

**A partial ASCII table (values are in decimal notation).**

| Value | Character | Value | Character | Value | Character |
|---|---|---|---|---|---|
| 32 | | 65 | A | 98 | b |
| 33 | ! | 66 | B | 99 | c |
| 34 | ” | 67 | C | 100 | d |
| 35 | # | 68 | D | 101 | e |
| 36 | $ | 69 | E | 102 | f |
| 37 | % | 70 | F | 103 | g |
| 38 | & | 71 | G | 104 | h |
| 39 | ’ | 72 | H | 105 | i |
| 40 | ( | 73 | I | 106 | j |
| 41 | ) | 74 | J | 107 | k |
| 42 | * | 75 | K | 108 | l |
| 43 | + | 76 | L | 109 | m |
| 44 | , | 77 | M | 110 | n |
| 45 | - | 78 | N | 111 | o |
| 46 | . | 79 | O | 112 | p |
| 47 | / | 80 | P | 113 | q |
| 48 | 0 | 81 | Q | 114 | r |
| 49 | 1 | 82 | R | 115 | s |
| 50 | 2 | 83 | S | 116 | t |
| 51 | 3 | 84 | T | 117 | u |
| 52 | 4 | 85 | U | 118 | v |
| 53 | 5 | 86 | V | 119 | w |
| 54 | 6 | 87 | W | 120 | x |
| 55 | 7 | 88 | X | 121 | y |
| 56 | 8 | 89 | Y | 122 | z |
| 57 | 9 | 90 | Z | 123 | { |
| 58 | : | 91 | [ | 124 | — |
| 59 | ; | 92 | | 125 | } |
| 60 | ¡ | 93 | ] | 126 | |
| 61 | = | 94 | | 127 | |
| 62 | ¿ | 95 | | | |
| 63 | ? | 96 | ‘ | | |
| 64 | @ | 97 | a | | |

# Glossary

**access time** the amount of time it takes for data requested from a device to become available.

**allocation unit** on certain versions of DOS an allocation unit is a group of bytes of fixed size (e.g., 2,048 bytes) that is locked out during low-level formatting if it contains a bad block.

**application programs** software written to solve specific problems such as payroll preparation, inventory, word processing, and so on.

**ASCII code** stands for American Standard Code for Information Interchange. It is a method whereby characters are stored using an 8-bit numeric code. See appendix.

**batch file** a file containing a series of DOS commands.

**bathtub curve** a graph that shows that the frequency of malfunctions in hardware components dramatically increases both very early and very late in the life of the component.

**baud** a data transmission rate in bits per second.

**binary expansion** method of representing integer numbers using only combinations of bits.

**binary search** a divide-and-conquer technique in which the range of the search is halved each time.

**bit** the basic unit of computer storage. A bit of memory can be either a "1" or a "0."

**boards** see *cards*.

**bootable disk** a disk that contains the boot portion of the operating system on it; also called a *system disk*.

**boot area** an area on a disk that contains a special code that allows the operating system to start.

**booting** the process of actually starting the computer's operating system.

**bootstrap code** special code stored in the boot area of a disk that allows the operating system to start.

**burn-in** letting the computer run for some extended period of time after it has been assembled to flush out major problems quickly.

**bus** the computer's internal system of wires. There are actually three types of busses in a microcomputer; the data bus, the address bus and the power bus.

**byte** 8 bits.

**cache memory** a technique of storing frequently used segments from the disk in fast memory on board a controller.

**CAD** computer aided design. A type of application program used in the design of various products.

**cards** computer components constructed of plastic laminates that hold dozens or even hundreds of chips and other electronic parts such as resistors, capacitors, transistors, and the like. Also called boards.

**carrier** the socket into which a chip is inserted. Sometimes called a chip pack.

**Centronics** a type of cable connector typically used by printers.

**chips** black "bug-like" pieces of plastic that contain thousands of small electronic circuits.

**clusters** DOS terminology for multiple sector units.

**CPU** central processing unit. The "brain" of the computer that performs all arithmetic and logical operations.

**cold boot** restarting the operating system by turning off and then turning on your computer.

**command processor** a program that displays the system prompt and processes user commands. It is stored in the command.com file in DOS.

**compacting** the process of defragmenting a disk. See *fragmentation*.

**contiguous files** files that are stored on disk without any unused space.

**controllers** devices that are used to transfer information between a peripheral and the CPU.

**control cable** special cable that connects a device to its controller, and passes control signals between them.

**coprocessor** a second independent microprocessor added to the computer to speed the execution of certain instructions, or extend the instruction set.

**crash** the event that occurs when a read/write head touches the surface of a platter. A crash usually causes irreparable damage to the disk.

**current** the rate of flow of electrons. Measured in amperes.

**cylinder** the collection of same-numbered tracks on a stack of disk platters.

**data cable** special cable that connects a device to its controller and passes data between them.

**daughterboard** a second board directly attached to the motherboard that enhances its performance, for example, from an XT to an AT.

**density** the amount of information that can be successfully stored per unit area on a disk.

**device drivers** software interfaces to special hardware.

**DIP switches** dual-in-line package switches. An array of rocker- or slider-type switches used to set certain system parameters. They are often used in place of setup programs on older systems.

**directory** a dictionary file kept by DOS containing information about files on your disk.

**display adapter** see *video card.*

**DMA** direct memory access. The transfer of data between the disk device and memory without the intervention of the CPU.

**DOS** disk operating system.

**dynamic** term used to describe memory that needs to be refreshed periodically due to gradual discharge.

**expanded memory** a technique that allows programs to use the 384K of memory normally reserved for the BIOS and screen memory.

**extended memory** memory that extends beyond the 1Mb logical limit of DOS.

**full-size cards** cards that are twice as long as half-size cards and might require a full-size slot on the motherboard. Also called full cards.

**floating point** operations performed on decimal numbers.

**fragmentation** the state wherein full and empty disk sectors are commingled in a checkerboard fashion on the disk. See Fig. 7-3.

**gender** the orientation on a cable connector—either female (holes) or male (pins).

**grounding straps** special bracelets used to connect your wrist to the computer chassis at all times in order to prevent buildup of harmful static electricity.

**half-size cards** short cards that plug into half-slots on the motherboard. Also called half cards.

**hidden files** files you cannot see with an ordinary DOS dir (directory) command.

**I/O devices** input/output devices. Also called *peripherals*.

**instruction set** the basic computation functions that can be performed by a CPU.

**interleave** a technique used to prevent data loss during transfer of data to/from a disk. Data is written to nonconsecutive sectors in order to allow the data transfer rate to keep up with the rotation speed of the disk.

**interrupts** special hardware signals that are used within the computer to indicate that some special operation is to be performed.

**interrupt requests** the process of issuing an interrupt.

**landing zone** a special track or cylinder where the disk heads are placed before shutting off power.

**logical** as "seen" by the microprocessor. (See *physical*).

**logical address space** the maximum memory or address space accessible by the microprocessor. Various schemes are used to map the logical address space into the physical address space.

**low-level formatting** the first step in the process of preparing a disk to receive data.

**magnetic domains** small magnets on the surface of disks and tapes. The orientation of the magnets represents either a binary "1" or "0."

**microcassettes** small, rigid diskettes. On some computers these take the place of floppy disks.

**microprocessor** the chip containing the CPU on the motherboard.

**minicomputers** small multiuser computers.

**modem** modulator/demodulator. A serial device that is used for transmitting information between computers over a phone line.

**monitor** the visual display or output device of the computer. Also called the screen.

**monochrome** single color, as in a monochrome monitor.

**motherboard** a large flat board inside the computer to which most of the basic components are connected.

**mouse** an input device consisting of a small roller ball in a hand-held casing that is used to move the cursor.

**multifunction card** a card that provides multiple functions, such as serial and/or parallel connections, clock/calendar, and additional memory.

**multimode** a device that is compatible with many other types of devices.

**multiport cards** cards that have multiple ports of a single type; for example, several parallel ports.

**nibble** 4 bits.

**null modem cable** a cable that allows two standard RS-232C devices to be connected directly without any other communications equipment such as a modem.

**operating system** a specialized collection of system programs that manage the physical resources of the computer. These programs work together in the same way regardless of which computer they are on.

**parking the disk** the process of placing the heads on the landing zone before shutting off power.

**partition** a logical section or drive of the hard disk.

**partition table** a disk file that contains information about how the disk is partitioned.

**path** an ordered list of directories that tells the system where to look for files. Also the current location within the directory tree.

**peripherals** devices used to put information into and get information out of the computer. Also called input/output devices.

**physical** as seen by the human. (See *logical*).

**physical address space** the total memory on board the system, which might be larger than the logical address space.

**platters** recording surfaces of the hard disk.

**populating** the process of adding chips to a card.

**port** an input/output channel for the computer.

**potential difference** the difference between the electron energy level on one side of a circuit and another (measured in volts). Also called a voltage.

**power** product of current and voltage, measured in watts.

**power supply** the physical unit in the computer that converts the current supplied from the wall receptacle to a form usable by the computer.

**primary port** the first port of a particular type in the computer.

**RAM** random access memory. Memory that can be both read from and written to.

**register** a special memory location that is internal to the CPU.

**ROM** read only memory. Memory that can be read but not destroyed, written over, or otherwise changed.

**screen** see monitor.

**secondary port** the second port of a particular type in the computer.
**setup programs** special programs provided with a computer to set or reset the system configuration parameters.
**shadow RAM** an area of RAM into which the BIOS is copied in order to speed operating system execution.
**SIMM** serial in-line memory module. A set of memory chips installed on a small PC board.
**software** special instructions for the computer.
**static** term used to describe memory that does not need to be refreshed periodically due to gradual discharge.
**straight through cable** a cable which allows a standard RS-232C device to be connected to communications equipment such as a modem.
**surge protector** a device used to protect the computer against sudden surges in power.
**system clock** clock internal to the CPU used for synchronization and timing.
**system programs** software used in the management of computer resources.
**throughput** the number of instructions or millions of instructions per second (MIPS) that can be performed by a CPU.
**trackball** a type of inverted mouse in which the casing is stationary while the ball moves.
**tracks** concentric circles on which data is organized sequentially on the disk.
**turbomouse** an input device that consists of a trackball and two buttons on a stationary pedestal.
**uninterruptible power supply** UPS. Essentially a large battery that can provide power for short periods of time.
**unpopulated cards** cards with no chips.
**VDU** visual display unit. The visual display or output device of the computer. (See *monitor.*)
**video card** a special board that interfaces the computer monitor to the computer. Also called a video display adapter.
**virtual split** the process of dividing a hard disk into more than one logical DOS drive.
**viruses** self-replicating programs transmitted via bulletin boards, disks of uncertain origin, and other means, that deliberately cause harm to a system's files.
**voltage** see potential difference.

**warm boot** restarting the operating system by pressing the reset button, if it exists, or pressing the Ctrl, Alt and Del keys simultaneously.

**words** groupings of bits. A word can have 8, 16, or more bits depending on the microprocessor.

# Bibliography


*AutoEGA User's Manual*, Richardson, Texas: STB Systems, Inc., 1988.

Brenner, Robert, C., *IBM Personal Computer Troubleshooting & Repair*, Indianapolis: Howard W. Sams & Company, 1989.

*MS-DOS User's Guide*, Fremont, California: Everex Systems, Inc., 1988.

*International Computer Dictionary*, Berkeley, California: Sybex, Inc., 1981.

*1330 PowerDrive Installation Manual*, Singapore: Micropolis Corporation, 1988.

*WDXT-GEN2 Quick Reference Guide*, Irvine, California: Western Digital Corp., 1989.

*MiniScribe Model 8438 30MB Fixed Disk Drive Installation Guide*, Austin, Texas: CompuAdd Corp., 1989.

*MS-DOS Shell User's Guide and User's Reference*, Austin, Texas: CompuAdd Corp., 1989.

*The Norton Trouble-Shooting Guide for Disks*, Santa Monica, California: Peter Norton Computing, Inc., 1988.

*The Norton Disk Companion*, Santa Monica, California: Peter Norton Computing, Inc., 1988.

*The Norton Utilities Advanced Edition Version 4.5*, Santa Monica, California: Peter Norton Computing, Inc., 1988.

Osborne, Adam, *Introduction to Microcomputers Vol. I: Basic Concepts, 2nd Edition*, Berkeley, California: Osborne/McGraw-Hill, 1980.

"Looking Back, Looking Ahead: CP/M, DOS, OS/2 and Windows," *PC Today*, Dec. 1990, pp. 16-20.

*Paradise Basic VGA Card Manual*, Mountain View, California: Western Digital Imaging/Paradise, 1989.

*Speedstore Software User's Guide*, San Jose, California: Software Dimensions, 1989.

*Universal Installation Handbook*, Scotts Valley, California: Seagate Technology, Inc., 1987.

*WD1002-27X Fixed Disk Controller Installation Guide*, Austin, Texas: CompuAdd Corp., 1989.

*WDXT-GEN2 Fixed Disk Controller Installation Guide*, Austin, Texas: CompuAdd Corp., 1989.

Williams, Gene, B., *How to Repair and Maintain Your IBM PC*, Radnor, Pennsylvania: Chilton Book Co., 1984.

# Index

## D



## E



## F



## G



## H



## I



## J



## K



## L

**Some typical hard disk sizes and their characteristics.**

| Disk size | Heads | Cylinders | Sectors/track | Disk size | Heads | Cylinders | Sectors/track |
|---|---|---|---|---|---|---|---|
| 10Mb | 4 | 306 | 17 | 71Mb | 10 | 823 | 17 |
| 21Mb | 3 | 820 | 17 | 71Mb | 8 | 1024 | 17 |
| 21Mb | 4 | 612 | 17 | 72Mb | 9 | 925 | 17 |
| 21Mb | 4 | 615 | 17 | 72Mb | 11 | 754 | 17 |
| 21Mb | 4 | 615 | 17 | 72Mb | 10 | 830 | 17 |
| 21Mb | 8 | 306 | 17 | 80Mb | 9 | 1024 | 17 |
| 25Mb | 3 | 987 | 17 | 85Mb | 5 | 969 | 36 |
| 31Mb | 5 | 733 | 17 | 88Mb | 4 | 1245 | 36 |
| 31Mb | 5 | 733 | 17 | 88Mb | 4 | 1249 | 36 |
| 31Mb | 5 | 733 | 17 | 98Mb | 11 | 1024 | 17 |
| 31Mb | 6 | 615 | 17 | 115Mb | 15 | 900 | 17 |
| 31Mb | 8 | 462 | 17 | 115Mb | 15 | 917 | 17 |
| 36Mb | 5 | 855 | 17 | 128Mb | 8 | 966 | 34 |
| 40Mb | 6 | 809 | 17 | 133Mb | 15 | 1024 | 17 |
| 42Mb | 5 | 977 | 17 | 137Mb | 10 | 823 | 34 |
| 42Mb | 5 | 977 | 17 | 144Mb | 8 | 1024 | 36 |
| 42Mb | 5 | 981 | 17 | 144Mb | 9 | 966 | 34 |
| 42Mb | 6 | 820 | 17 | 151Mb | 7 | 1225 | 36 |
| 42Mb | 7 | 699 | 17 | 151Mb | 7 | 1224 | 36 |
| 42Mb | 7 | 733 | 17 | 153Mb | 7 | 1245 | 36 |
| 42Mb | 8 | 615 | 17 | 153Mb | 9 | 969 | 36 |
| 44Mb | 5 | 1024 | 17 | 154Mb | 7 | 1249 | 36 |
| 44Mb | 7 | 733 | 17 | 159Mb | 15 | 1224 | 17 |
| 46Mb | 7 | 754 | 17 | 161Mb | 8 | 1147 | 36 |
| 48Mb | 6 | 940 | 17 | 166Mb | 8 | 1216 | 35 |
| 50Mb | 7 | 830 | 17 | 223Mb | 9 | 1412 | 36 |
| 51Mb | 5 | 989 | 17 | 249Mb | 12 | 1216 | 35 |
| 51Mb | 7 | 855 | 17 | 321Mb | 15 | 1218 | 36 |
| 55Mb | 7 | 918 | 17 | 323Mb | 15 | 1224 | 36 |
| 56Mb | 7 | 925 | 17 | 323Mb | 15 | 1225 | 36 |
| 58Mb | 7 | 977 | 17 | 372Mb | 15 | 1412 | 36 |
| 60Mb | 7 | 1024 | 17 | | | | |
| 61Mb | 7 | 1024 | 17 | | | | |
| 64Mb | 8 | 940 | 17 | | | | |